CW00823169

SKI MAGIC© 'the secrets of skiing explained'

COPYRIGHT: © 1997 Roger Bays
TEXT; GRAPHICS; PAGE LAYOUT & COVER DESIGN: Roger Bays
PUBLISHED BY: Squaremoon Creations©
FIRST PUBLISHED: 1997
ISBN: 0-9583661-0-1
PRINTED BY: The Caxton Press, Christchurch, New Zealand

DISCLAIMER
Skiing inherently involves risk of personal injury and damage to property. Skiers have widely varying levels of ability and of fitness. While the author has used due care in the preparation of this book he does not give any warranty that the advice given will be appropriate for any skier in any particular circumstance. The author hereby disclaims any liability in law equity or otherwise for any claims for any injury or damage arising directly or indirectly as a result of following advice given in this book or arising in any way as a result of the publication of this book.

ORDERING BOOKS

The following products are available by mail order:
1. Ski Magic.
2. Ski Magic in large print.
3. Individual Ski Magic pages and bulk order pages for educational groups.

Browse the Ski Magic **world wide web site**, for up-to-date information on Ski Magic and other ski books and products from Squaremoon Creations.

FOR UP-TO-DATE INFORMATION SHEET~PRICES~ORDERING

web: browse the animated Ski Magic web site at:
http://www.mailhost.net/~skimagic
http://www.mailhost.net/~squaremoon

e-mail: skimagic@mailhost.net

post: Ski Magic
Squaremoon Creations
PO Box 13522, Christchurch, New Zealand

phone+fax: dial directory enquires for current number of
Squaremoon Creations, Christchurch, New Zealand.

ACKNOWLEDGEMENTS

ALEC & VAL SCARESBROOK~Thanks for the many hours you have put into proof-reading this book. Your work has helped convey the message more clearly. And thanks for all the advice along the way.

MUM & DAD~Thanks for all your help and support while in England. Your help enabled me to finish the book in time for the winter season.

DR ANDREW BLELOCH~Thanks for checking over the physics content, and for the insights and comments. Some key points came up in our chats.

JOHN NEWCOMBE~Thanks for all the help you gave me, and for explaining the desktop publishing process from disk to printing. You saved me an incredible amount of time and energy by explaining all the steps along the way.

MARK McKINSTRY~Thanks for taking me through the explanation of the building blocks that make up a computer system. This proved to be so very helpful in choosing a machine for producing this book. And thanks for answering all the computer-related questions that followed.

ROBIN GRAHAM~Thanks for all the time you spent teaching me the ins and outs of English grammar; it was a pleasure to be taught by you. Hope you don't find too many mistakes.

DR MIKE CLARK~Thanks for explaining HTML to me and helping me to create an animated web site.

JOHNNY YOUNG~Thanks for all your help with the final checks and for your honest feedback.

PETER WOOLLEY GRAPHICS LTD, CHRISTCHURCH, NEW ZEALAND~Thanks for the advice on computers and graphics systems. The advice to use a PC based computer saved me a lot of money on hardware and software.

MICROMART COMPUTERS, CHRISTCHURCH, NEW ZEALAND~Thanks to all the staff for all their help in the early days of setting up my computer system. Also for the continued backup and support. I appreciated the friendly and helpful service.

SNELL SPORTS, CHAMONIX, FRANCE~Thanks Olivia, Hiroshi and the rest of the staff for your help while in Chamonix.

OTHER PEOPLE AND ORGANISATIONS WHO GAVE THEIR HELP~Andi McCann; Graham Morgan; Tom Lachlan-Cope; Liz Morris; Maryanne Tipler; Mike Dunn; Geoff Phelps; Dee Clarke; Alison Brizzell; Joe Tanner; Yasmin Zabidin; Jane Cameron; Neil Sloan; Chamonix Valley Ski Area; The Ski Exchange Ltd, Cambridge, England; Bassingbourne Ski Centre, England.

Also many thanks to my friends who gave me encouragement and support during this project.

DEDICATION

the snow and terrain are our teachers
the snow and terrain are our teachers
the snow and terrain are our teachers
the snow and terrain are our teachers
the snow and terrain are our teachers

to all skiers

the snow and terrain are our teachers
the snow and terrain are our teachers
the snow and terrain are our teachers
the snow and terrain are our teachers
the snow and terrain are our teachers
the snow and terrain are our teachers

READING THIS BOOK

I have designed this book to make the most sense when read from front to back. Some people may want to read individual chapters out of sequence; some chapters lend themselves to this, others don't. Here are a few guidelines:

  Chapters one, six and seven can be read out of sequence because they don't rely too heavily on previous knowledge.

  Read chapters two to five in order, even if you are an expert skier or competitor, as these chapters build on each other in use of terms and ideas.

1. Basic Techniques

2. How Skis Work
3. Parallel Turn
4. Snow Techniques   *read in sequence*
5. Terrain Techniques

6. Ski Equipment
7. Fixing Ski Gear

TRY NOW

Take responsibility for your own safety as you try these exercises

TRY NOW EXERCISE
As you go through chapter three (on the parallel turn) you will find a series of TRY NOW exercises.

The aims of the exercises are to:
1. Bring clarity to the body movements being described.
2. Reinforce your memory of each movement.
3. Check your understanding.
4. Help you visualise the position.
5. Allow your body to **feel** the position.
6. Give you an insight into what is happening as you ski.

READING THIS BOOK

TITLE BAR
The title bar shows you exactly where you are in the book.

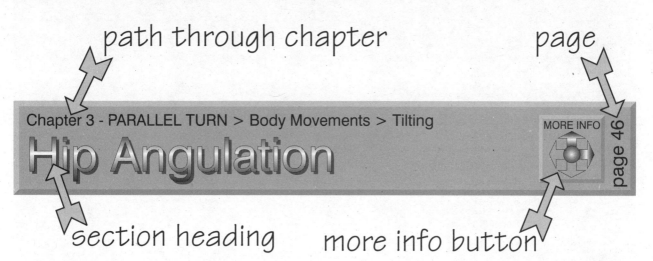

path through chapter

page

Chapter 3 - PARALLEL TURN > Body Movements > Tilting

Hip Angulation

MORE INFO

page 46

section heading

more info button

MORE INFO BUTTON
The role of the 'more info' button is to give you a better idea of where you are in the book.

   The **horizontal** arrows show you if there are more pages with the same section heading on a previous or following page.

   The **vertical** arrows show you if there is a subchapter level above or below.

   The arrows are either highlighted (shiny) or greyed (dull).

when highlighted,
a higher level exists

when highlighted,
previous pages at
same level exists

MORE INFO

when highlighted,
further pages at
same level exists

when highlighted,
a lower level exists

CONTENTS

BOOK INFORMATION
ACKNOWLEDGEMENTS
DEDICATION
READING THIS BOOK

CONTENTS

The Fall Line
Snowplough Technique
   Snowplough Brake
   Snowplough Turn
   Snowplough Stop
Straight Running
Side-Slipping
Side-Stepping
Herringboning
Skating Step
Traversing
The Tuck
Kick Turn
Hockey Stop

This chapter explains the basic ski techniques. These enable you to make the basic ski manoeuvres to get around a ski resort. They include braking, turning, stopping, accelerating, sliding, climbing, skating, traversing and turning around on the spot.

  The techniques are used by all levels of skier and do not become redundant as you progress.

The fall line is the path that skiers follow as they descend a slope. Once you recognise the fall line, you can use it to pick out the more interesting and fun lines down the mountain.

WHAT IS THE FALL LINE?

One way to picture the fall line is to imagine standing on a mountain slope and rolling an orange down it. Gravity causes the orange to take the steepest path. The path the orange takes (provided it doesn't gather too much speed) is the fall line. From any point on a mountain there is only one path that the orange would follow.

Another way to picture the fall line is to imagine walking down a hillside with your back to the slope. You are now following the fall line. Turning side on to the slope as you walk takes you out of the fall line. You are now traversing the slope instead.

WHY FOLLOW THE FALL LINE?

Following the fall line enables your left and right turns to be symmetrical. This allows you to ski with an even rhythm. Taking a line that wanders off the fall line may feel awkward because your left turns will be different from your right turns.

FALL LINES DRAWN ON A CONTOUR MAP

Fall lines drawn on a contour map always cross the contour lines at ninety degrees. The contour map below shows the different fall lines from four start points near the summit of a mountain. Note that the fall line is seldom a straight line.

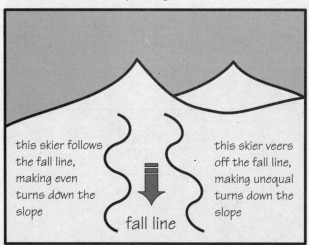

this skier follows the fall line, making even turns down the slope

this skier veers off the fall line, making unequal turns down the slope

fall line

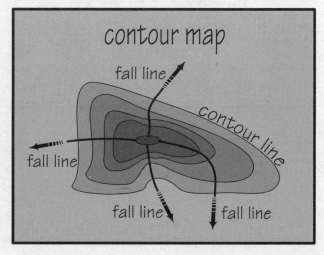

contour map

fall line

contour line

fall line

fall line

fall line

The snowplough technique enables you to get around many parts of a ski resort with a little practice. It is an extremely versatile technique that works in most situations and snow conditions. One basic body position enables you to **brake**, **turn** and **stop**.

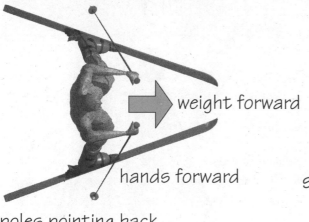

weight forward

hands forward

poles pointing back

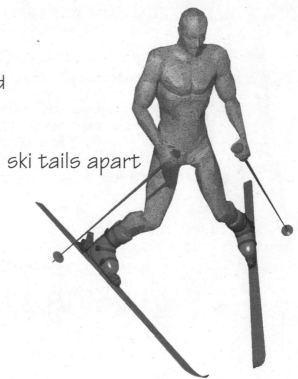

ski tails apart

ski tips together

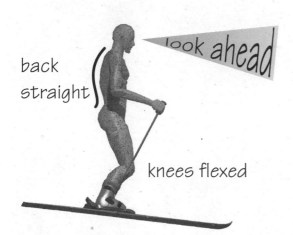

back straight

look ahead

knees flexed

POLES
Poles don't have to be planted in any of the snowplough techniques. Use them when necessary to aid balance.

Snowplough Brake

The snowplough brake slows you down. It also stops you on gentle slopes.

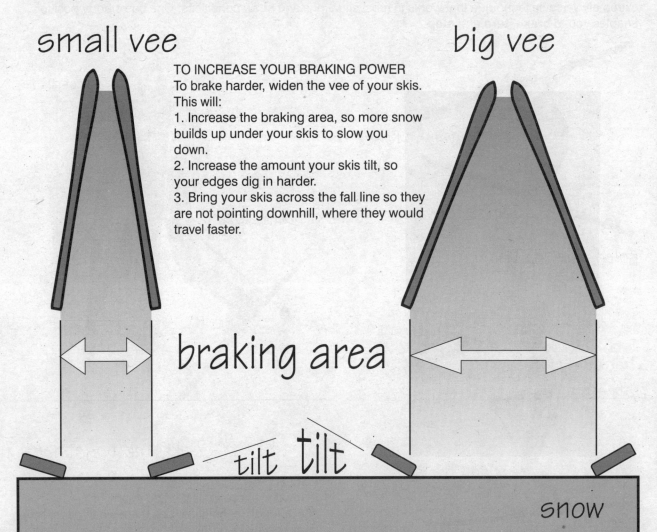

small vee

big vee

TO INCREASE YOUR BRAKING POWER
To brake harder, widen the vee of your skis.
This will:
1. Increase the braking area, so more snow builds up under your skis to slow you down.
2. Increase the amount your skis tilt, so your edges dig in harder.
3. Bring your skis across the fall line so they are not pointing downhill, where they would travel faster.

braking area

tilt tilt

snow

Snowplough Turn

The snowplough turn gives you manoeuvrability and additional braking.

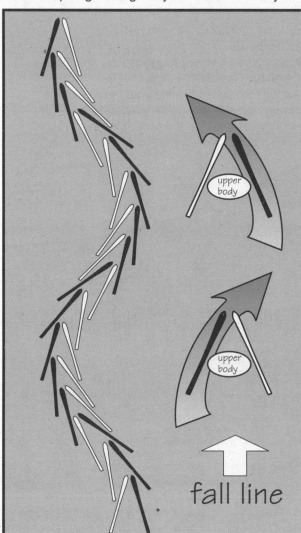

upper body

upper body

fall line

TURNING IN EITHER DIRECTION

Shifting your weight from one ski to the other enables you to turn in either direction. Once you have more weight on one ski, that ski will turn automatically.

To turn to the **left,** put your weight on your **right** ski, while keeping your upper body central

unweighted ski

weighted ski

To turn to the **right,** put your weight on your **left** ski, while keeping your upper body central

UPPER BODY POSITION CENTRAL

Your skis turn because they are **tilted** against the snow's surface. When transferring weight onto one ski, keep your body central. If you lean your body over toward the weighted ski, you will flatten it against the snow, causing it to travel in a straight line rather than an arc.

Snowplough Stop

The snowplough brake can stop you on gentle slopes. On steeper slopes, however, you need to use the snowplough stop to bring you to rest. The snowplough stop works by bringing your skis across the slope, so they are not pointing down the fall line.

TECHNIQUE
From the basic snowplough stance, weight one ski so you turn across the slope.

As the turn finishes, slide your inside ski (the unweighted ski) alongside your outside ski (the weighted ski making the turn). Stop with your skis side by side across the slope.

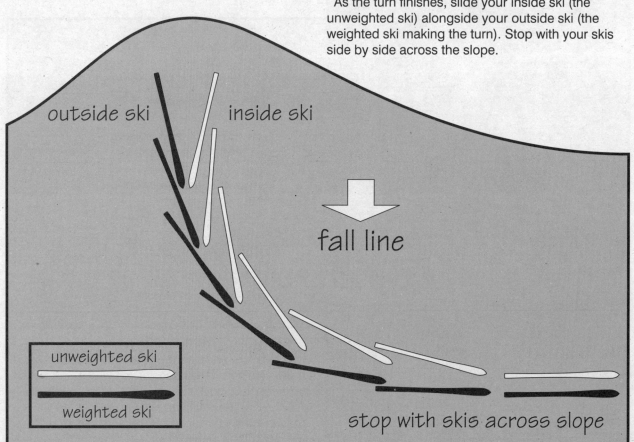

outside ski   inside ski

fall line

unweighted ski

weighted ski

stop with skis across slope

Straight running (also known as schussing) is skiing in a straight line.

BODY POSITION

Position your skis hip-width apart, with the bases flat on the snow. Stand with your knees flexed and your weight slightly forward. Your weight is forward when you can feel your shins against the tongue of your ski boots. Adjust the position of your weight fore and aft to compensate for changes in the terrain.

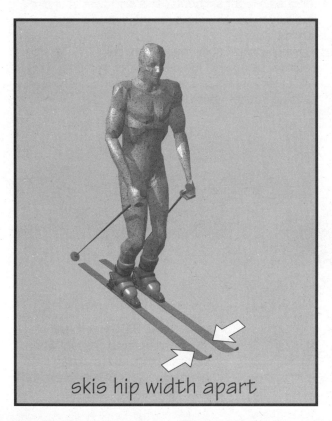

skis hip width apart

SAFE RUN OUT

Practice is safer on a gentle slope with a good **run out** (a large flat area below you where you can guarantee to stop).

If you need to slow down or stop, revert to the snowplough brake or the snowplough stop.

CATCHING AN EDGE

The expression 'catching an edge' describes the situation where one of your ski edges catches in the snow, causing it to veer off to the side. It is sometimes possible to recover from this by momentarily transferring all your weight onto the ski that is tracking correctly and repositioning the other ski.

WEIGHT BACK AT LOW SPEED

On cat tracks (a snow covered roadway around the side of a mountain, that snow grooming machines drive on) or very gentle slopes that are so flat that you hardly move forward, you can increase your speed by moving your weight backward on your skis. Do this by pressing your calf muscles against the backs of your boots. When you do this your speed will pick up. The trade off is that the tips of your skis will skitter around a little, causing a loss in stability. At low speeds this is not usually a problem.

THE PIKE

To schuss in the 'pike' position, bend a little at the waist and cross your hands behind your back. This cuts down air resistance, enabling you to ski faster.

Side-Slipping

Side-slipping enables you to negotiate steep or narrow sections of the mountain where you cannot safely or practically descend by a turning technique. It's a good skill to develop early, as once learnt it can get you past sections that you are finding difficult, with a greater degree of safety than using a turning technique.

TECHNIQUE

To side-slip, position your skis across the fall line. The idea is to let your skis slide **sideways** down the slope.

To start your skis sliding, push your knees away from the slope. This puts your skis onto their bases so they can slide freely.

To stop, push your knees toward the slope, putting your skis back on their edges, which dig in and prevent you sliding further.

AVOIDING OBSTACLES

To avoid obstacles, you need to be able to creep forward or backward as you descend.

To move forward, bring your weight forward on your skis by pressing your shins against the tongues of your ski boots. This will lower your ski tips as you continue to descend, moving you forward.

To move back, shift your weight back by pressing your calves against the rear of your ski boots. This will lower your ski tails as you continue to descend, causing you to move backward.

twist upper body toward fall line so you can see where you are going

move knees into slope to stop

move knees away from slope to start moving

fall line

diagonal side slipping

DIAGONAL SIDE-SLIPPING

To speed up your descent when side-slipping, take a zigzag path by rocking your weight back and forth as you descend.

Side-stepping enables you to **ascend** a ski slope.

TECHNIQUE
Start Position:
Place your skis across the fall line.
Sequence:
Ascend the slope taking small steps upward. Use your poles for balance.

POLES
You may find it helpful to change your grip on your **downhill** pole. Holding the end of the handle makes it easier to push against, particularly when on a steep slope.

DIAGONAL SIDE-STEPPING
You may prefer to move up and slightly forward with each step, to give a more natural movement. Remember this when you start the climb so you end up where you want to go.

fall line

step up slope diagonally

The herringbone technique enables you to **ascend** gentle slopes more quickly and easily than side-stepping. However, as the steepness of a slope increases, side-stepping becomes a more efficient technique to use. Medium to steep slopes are impossible to climb using the herringbone technique. The name herringboning derives from the fish-bone pattern left in the snow by the skis.

TECHNIQUE
Start Position:
Face up the fall line with your ski tips apart and tails together.
Sequence:
Ascend the slope taking small steps forward.
 Lift your opposite ski and pole together for a natural motion.
 Push against your poles to help you climb.

FACE UP THE FALL LINE
Facing up the fall line allows you to progress with an even rhythm.
 Ascending at an angle to the fall line may feel awkward.

EDGES
Use your skis' inside edges for grip by pushing your knees inward, so you don't slip back.

GRIP END OF POLES
You may find it helpful to change your grip and hold the end of the poles. This gives a little extra usable length to your poles, making them easier to push against.

ski tails together

ski tips apart

fall line

Skating Step

The skating step enables you to cross a flat section of snow, or ski down a gently sloping section with more speed than with other techniques. For the energetic, it can be used to ascend gentle slopes. It is similar to the herringbone technique except that your skis glide across the snow with each step forward.

TECHNIQUE
The technique is the same as that used in ice-skating, roller-skating and in-line skating.

Start Position:
Position your skis so that the ski tips are apart, and ski tails are together.

Sequence:
Right Glide
1. Step your right ski forward by pushing against your left ski. At the same time thrust your right hand and shoulder forward to assist the motion.
2. Switch weight from your left ski onto your right ski and catch the free ride as it glides over the snow.

Left Glide
1. Step your left ski forward by pushing against your right ski. At the same time thrust your left hand and shoulder forward to assist the motion.
2. Switch weight from your right ski onto your left ski and catch the free ride as it glides over the snow.

<Repeat right left sequence to continue>

Note: Rather than thrusting an arm forward when gliding, you can instead plant both poles together and push against them. You may find it is easier to plant poles with alternate glides (e.g. every right glide), rather than with each glide.

WHERE TO PRACTICE
The skating step is a tiring manoeuvre to learn on flat snow. If you practise the movement down a slight incline, gravity will help you glide.

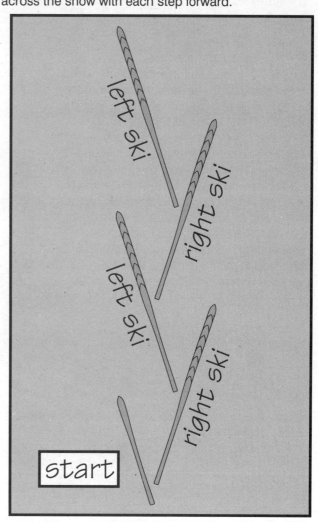

Traversing

Traversing enables you to skirt around the mountainside. The techniques described here are for traversing using a ski-width track, or no track at all.
 When traversing using a cat track, you can use snowploughing, straight running or tucking (see page 14), depending on steepness.

HEIGHT AND SPEED
Skiers usually want to traverse a slope with reasonable speed and maintain their height on the slope. Unfortunately, a compromise has to be made between traversing with speed and losing height rapidly, or traversing slowly and retaining more height.
 Losing height may mean that at the end of the traverse you are below the point you need to be and have to side-step up, or you have missed out on a lot of good skiing that is now above you. Travelling slowly to keep high can be frustrating and impractical.
 Developing a good traversing technique helps you to maintain height whilst travelling with reasonable speed.

TRAVERSE POSITION
When traversing, your skis are across the slope and, given half a chance, will slip down it. You can prevent this by:
1. Keeping most of your weight on your downhill ski.
2. Pushing your knees toward the slope, so your skis' edges bite into it. (Note that your legs must be bent to do this).
3. Skiing with your uphill ski in front, so the downhill ski tip acts as a guard, stopping your uphill ski from crossing over it. This reduces the likelihood of a fall.

knees into slope

uphill ski in front

most of weight on downhill ski

fall line

step up

STEPPING UP IN THE TRAVERSE
One way to gain height is to take small steps up while traversing.

Traversing

SKATING IN THE TRAVERSE

One way to gain more speed in the traverse is to use a skating step as you follow the track. This also helps you to maintain height.

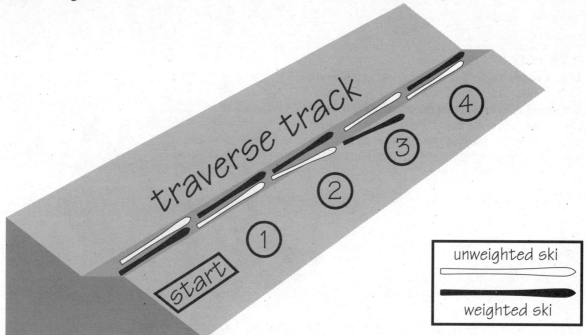

| unweighted ski |
| weighted ski |

SKATING TECHNIQUE IN A TRAVERSE

Start Position:

Start from the normal traverse position with most of your weight on the downhill ski.

Sequence:

1. Transfer your weight onto your uphill ski.
2. Point your downhill ski off to the side of the traverse line.
3. Transfer your weight onto your downhill ski (this will cause you to accelerate).
4. Now transfer your weight quickly onto your uphill ski before it leaves the original traverse track, while returning your downhill ski to the track.

   <Repeat steps 2,3,4 to continue >

The tuck (also known as the egg) enables you to ski faster in a straight line by making you more aerodynamic than in the straight running position.

BODY POSITION
Take a wide stance with your feet, and place your elbows near your knees. Let your ski poles sit alongside your waist, resting on your hips. Your skis should sit flat on the snow. Position your weight slightly forward, so your shins press against the tongues of your boots. Make adjustments to weight position to suit the terrain.

wide stance

The kick turn enables you to turn around and face the opposite direction from a standing position. It has an amusing quality to it, particularly for whoever is coaching the manoeuvre. It is often learnt when needed as a way of getting out of a tight spot; this is usually where most of the amusement occurs. If you can practise this in advance, you may be the one who is smiling when you need to use it.

TECHNIQUE
Start Position:
Position your skis across the fall line, so you will not slide forward or backward. Plant both poles for stability.
Sequence:
1. **Skis -** In one fluid motion, swing your downhill leg so you can plant the tail of the ski next to the tip of the uphill ski. Getting the tail of the ski as far forward as possible makes the following movements all the easier.
Poles - Move the downhill pole behind your back, and uphill of both your skis.
2. **Skis only -** Rotate the downhill leg so the tip of the downhill ski is alongside the tail of the uphill ski, then transfer your weight onto the downhill ski.
3. **Poles -** Remove the pole on the side of your uphill leg.
Skis - Bring your uphill ski around to sit below your other ski.

Your skis are now either side by side and facing the new direction or they are in a tangled mess! Have fun.

MAKING IT EASY
1. You may find it easier to complete the sequence in one flowing motion.
2. The kick turn is learnt more easily on a flat section of snow.

start position

fall line

1

2

3

Hockey Stop

The hockey stop enables you to halt quickly and effectively.

TECHNIQUE
Start Position:
Start from skiing slowly down a gentle slope.
Sequence:
1. Bend your legs, then extend them. This eases your weight off your skis.
2. With your weight momentarily off your skis, use your legs to swing your skis across the slope.
3. As your weight comes back on your skis, angle your knees into the slope so the ski edges bite in.

SAFETY NOTE
When stopping next to others, stop on the **downhill** side. That way, if you lose control as you brake, you won't crash into them.

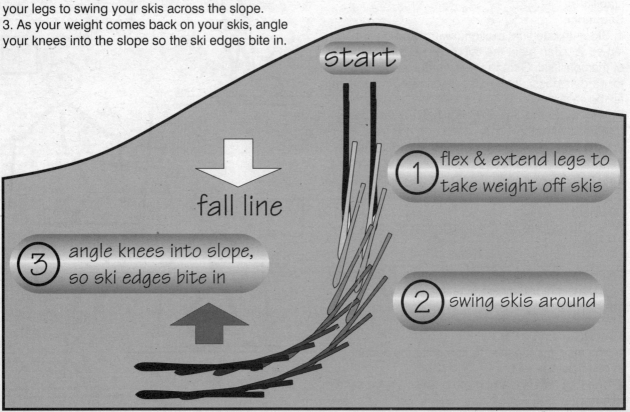

start

fall line

1 flex & extend legs to take weight off skis

3 angle knees into slope, so ski edges bite in

2 swing skis around

This chapter explains how your skis work in the snow. Knowing this can help you make sense of the descriptions of body movements for the various turning techniques. This is particularly so for the parallel turn, which is more complex than the snowplough turn.

When skiing, you do two basic things:

1. Steering: Steering your skis enables you to go where you want and avoid obstacles. Steering is achieved by using straight running and turning techniques.

2. Braking: Braking enables you to slow down to a manageable speed, so you can maintain your balance. Braking is achieved through making turns.

GOLDEN RULES OF SKIING

All straight running and turning techniques rely on two principles.

1. A straight ski follows a straight line.

2. A bent ski follows an arc.

  By learning to control the shape of your skis, you can steer and brake.

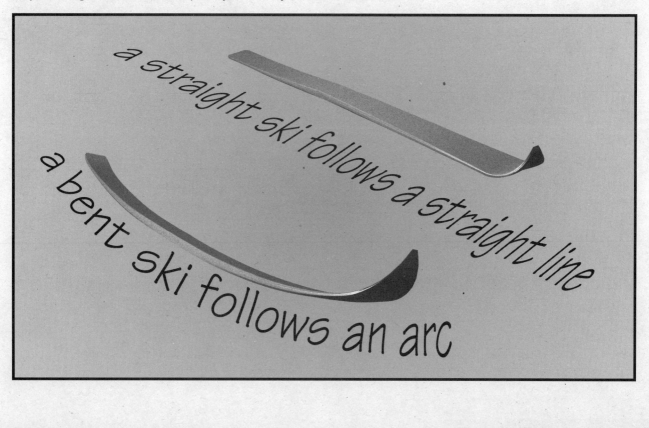

Steering

To steer your skis in a straight line, you must keep them **flat** on the snow and **press** your weight onto them. To steer your skis in an arc, you must **tilt** them against the snow and **press** your weight onto them. The combination of tilting your skis and applying your weight causes them to flex. This enables the ski to follow a curved path. The more the ski is tilted, the tighter it will turn. All turning techniques rely on tilting the ski to change its shape.

flat + press = straight running ski	tilt + press = turning ski

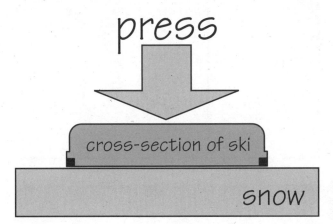

edge cuts a groove into snow

WHY DO YOUR SKIS FLEX WHEN TILTED?
Skis flex when tilted because the side of the ski is curved. This feature is called sidecut. Later in this chapter you can read in detail about sidecut (see pages 25-7).

CUTTING YOUR OWN TRACK
When a train follows a curved railway track, the track guides the train around the bend.

In skiing, your skis are bent to the curve of the turn and your edges cut a groove through the snow. You cut your own track as you go.

Braking

Turning brakes you by displacing snow and decreasing the path angle.

BRAKING BY DISPLACING SNOW
This is the main way you brake. As your skis dig in during a turn, they **compress** and **move** snow sideways, creating a plume of snow thrown up from your skis. The work done (energy used) in compressing and moving this snow slows you down.

BRAKING BY DECREASING PATH ANGLE
Making turns down a slope means that you travel a **longer distance** to get to the bottom than when skiing straight down the slope. Travelling further (a longer path length) for the same loss in height means that the **average angle** that you are descending must be **less**. Skiing a less steep slope means you accelerate less, causing you to travel more slowly.

Racers try to minimise the amount they turn because turning decreases speed and increases the distance to the finish line, which increases their time.

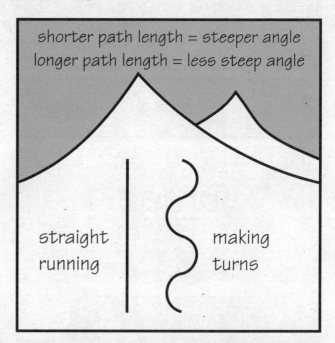

shorter path length = steeper angle
longer path length = less steep angle

straight running

making turns

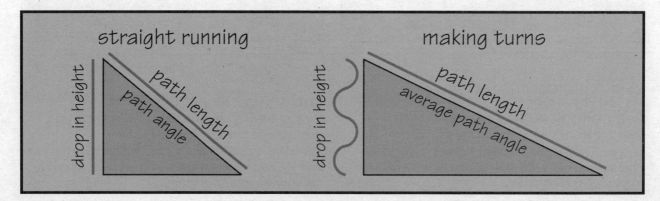

straight running

drop in height

path length

path angle

making turns

drop in height

path length

average path angle

Ski Design

MORE INFO

This section explains the parts that make up a ski, and the attributes that enable it to function.

parts	attributes
shovel	sidecut
waist	camber
tip	taper angle
tail	flex
edges	torsional stiffness
top-sheet	swing weight
sidewalls	
core	
base	
base reinforcement	
binding reinforcement	

A NOTE ON SKI VIBRATION

Skis vibrate as they run over the snow. The harder and rougher the surface, and the greater your speed, the more they will vibrate. E.g. a hard icy surface will cause your skis to vibrate (chatter) as you ski over it.

A ski that is vibrating has intermittent contact with the snow at the tip and tail, causing it to feel unstable. This affects the tracking of the ski because it will try to veer off course unpredictably. Poor tracking makes it harder to keep the ski pointing in the direction that you wish to go.

Skis are most prone to vibration when travelling in a straight line. In a turn, the tension of the flexed skis helps to reduce vibration.

Camber, flex (discussed later in this section on pages 28 & 30), and careful use of material in the construction of skis, help to reduce vibration.

Vibrating skis are the bane of skiers and ski designers.

Parts of the Ski

MORE INFO

Skis consist of many parts. Each part contributes to the overall functioning of the ski.

SHOVEL
The shovel of the ski is the widest part. The extra width helps the ski to float rather than sink when used in deep soft snow.

WAIST
The waist of the ski is the narrowest part and is close to the middle of the ski.

shovel: the widest part of the ski

waist: the narrowest part of the ski

tip: the point of the ski

tail: the rear half of the ski

TIP
The tip is pointed and curved upward. This design prevents the ski digging into the snow as you ski.

TAIL
The tail of the ski is the part of the ski behind the rear ski binding.

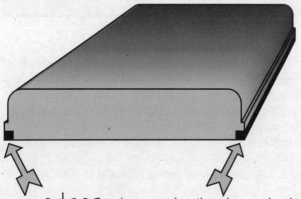

EDGES
Edges are the strips of steel along the base of the ski. Their role is to give grip to the ski when used on a firm surface.

edges: the steel rails along the length of the ski

TOP-SHEET & SIDEWALLS
Traditionally, the top-sheet and sidewalls of skis are manufactured from separate parts and bonded together. A more recent 'cap' technique consists of a single moulded construction. Both methods are currently used. Their role is to encase the core in a protective durable material and give strength to the ski.

TRADITIONAL CONSTRUCTION
Using traditional construction techniques, the ski is made up from a core surrounded by a top-sheet, sidewalls, a base-reinforcing layer, and the ski base.

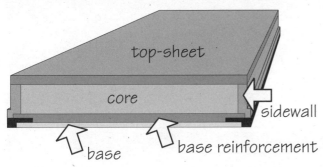

CAP CONSTRUCTION
The top and sides of cap skis are made from one moulded construction. The ski still has a separate core, base-reinforcing layer, and ski base.

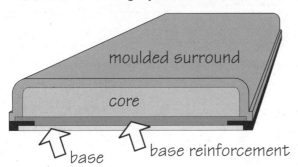

CORE
The core of skis can be made from a variety of materials. Usually, foam or laminated wood and fibreglass form the bulk of the core, with smaller quantities of more exotic materials. The materials and construction chosen must allow the ski to **flex,** and have properties that **dampen vibration**. As with other parts of the ski, the core has to be **durable** and **resilient** so the ski will continue to bend back to its original shape after each turn.
 Here are the basic configurations:
Laminate/sandwich: Strips of wood laminated together.
Torsion box: Wood laminated and wrapped in fibreglass.
Foam fill: Filled with foam.

BINDING REINFORCEMENT LAYER
The ski must be suitably strong internally under the binding area, to hold the binding screws.

BASE & BASE REINFORCEMENT
The base provides the running surface that the ski slides on. Bases should have a low coefficient of friction so they slide easily on the snow. Bases should also be able to absorb waxes, which are applied to reduce friction further.
 The base reinforcement layer gives a firm backing to the base so it maintains its shape.

Ski Attributes

Skis have a number of attributes that enable them to run straight or turn. Slight differences in these properties give skis a particular character and feel when skied.

Attributes:
Sidecut - the arc that makes the ski's waist the narrowest part of the ski.
Camber - the arch under the ski.
Taper Angle - the angle from tail to shovel.
Flex - the lengthways stiffness of the ski.
Torsional Stiffness - the amount of resistance to twisting along the length of the ski
Swing Weight - the rotational weight of the ski.

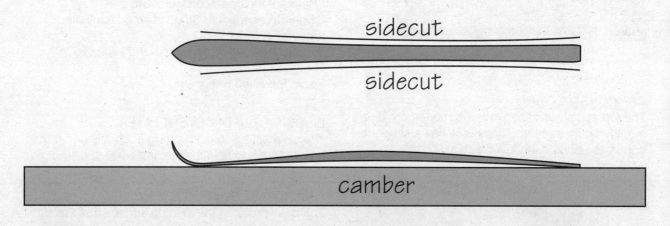

Sidecut is the narrowing of the ski near its centre. Its role is to help skis flex so they can turn. Sidecut facilitates turning in two ways, depending on whether you are skiing on firm, or through soft, snow. Both work on the principle that if you support the ski at either end it will bend under your weight, and the forces of the turn. In each case, you have to tilt the ski rather than keep it flat on the snow.

CUT-OUT SKIS

To help you understand sidecut, two skis have been printed on the inside rear cover of this book. Please cut them out and experiment.

ski with no sidecut

ski with sidecut

HOW TO MAKE A SKI TRACK IN A STRAIGHT LINE

Before looking at how sidecut helps a ski flex so it can turn, it is helpful to see how to make your skis track in a straight line.

If you take the cut-out skis and place them **flat** on a table top, you will notice that it is impossible to bend either ski by pressing directly onto it. The table, which represents the snow, supports the skis and keeps them straight. As the skis cannot bend they have to track in a straight line.

When you want to travel in a straight line, you must keep your skis flat on the snow, by keeping your legs directly under your body.

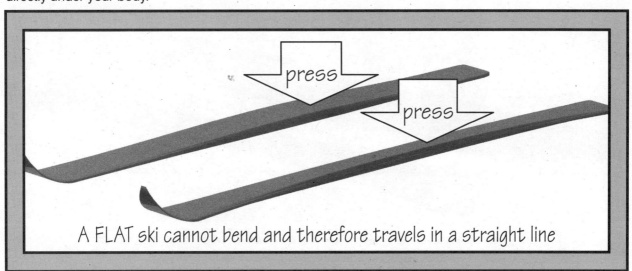

press

press

A FLAT ski cannot bend and therefore travels in a straight line

SIDECUT AND FIRM SNOW

Take the cut-out ski **with sidecut** from the back of the book and tilt it against the surface of a table. Notice how a gap forms under the centre of the ski as it touches the table at the tip and tail.

If you now press on the top surface of the ski it will flex.

The more you tilt the ski, the bigger the gap between the centre of the ski and the table, and the more the ski can flex. The more the ski is flexed, the tighter it is able to turn.

Now tilt the ski with **no sidecut**. Notice how no gap forms. The edge touches the table along its whole length, making it difficult for the ski to bend. The only way a ski with no sidecut can flex is by compressing and displacing snow underneath it. For this to happen the snow would need to be soft rather than hard like the table. Skis do flex further than the sidecut allows as there is always some compression and displacement of snow under the ski.

When you want to turn, you must tilt your skis so they can flex by moving your legs out to the side of your body. With the snowplough turn, you move your legs to opposite sides. With the parallel turn, you move both legs to the same side.

ski with no sidecut

ski with sidecut

gap

A TILTED ski can bend and therefore travels in an arc

Sidecut

MORE INFO

SIDECUT AND DEEP SOFT SNOW

When turning on firm snow, your skis ride on their edges, and your weight is supported only along the edges of the skis. When turning in deep soft snow, your skis compress the snow under the base, forming a platform that they slide against.

In deep snow, the effect sidecut has in helping the ski to flex is minimal. A ski without sidecut would still flex. Sidecut does, however, facilitate flexing by providing a larger surface area at the tip and tail to support your weight. This encourages more flexing in the middle of the ski where it is narrower.

In soft snow, the degree of **flex** plays the greater role in bending the ski.

only edge of ski touches snow

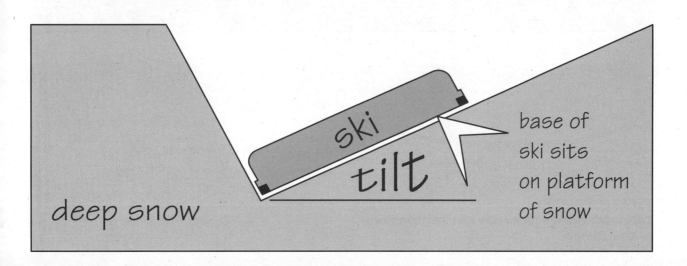

larger surface area at tip and tail of ski

deep snow

base of ski sits on platform of snow

Camber

Camber is the arch in the ski. Its role is to help ensure that the full length of the ski is in contact with the snow when travelling in a straight line. This helps dampen vibration in the ski to give better tracking and stability.

CAMBER ACTS LIKE A SPRING

Camber helps dampen vibration by acting like a spring, and pinning down the tip and the tail of the ski when you place your weight on it. This ensures that the tip and tail are in good contact with the snow.

Can you visualise how a ski with no camber would be more prone to vibration at the tip and tail?

Camber is most effective at reducing vibration when skiing in a straight line. In a turn, the ski is bent to such a degree that the benefits of camber are minimal in comparison with the other forces on the ski.

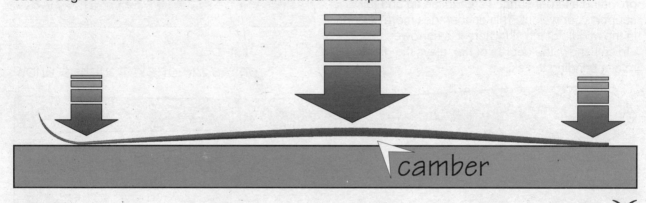

camber

reverse camber

TO SEE CAMBER

Camber can most easily be seen when both skis are placed base to base. The strength of the camber can be felt by squeezing the skis together with your thumb and forefinger.

REVERSE CAMBER

When your skis are bent in the turn they bend into reverse camber.

Taper Angle

Taper angle helps initiation of turns. It also reduces sidewall drag when travelling in a straight line.

taper angle

TAPER ANGLE ADVANCES THE TURN

To understand how taper angle helps you initiate each turn, it is helpful to imagine what would happen if your skis were narrower at the shovel instead of wider. The diagram shows three skis, one with a wide shovel, another of equal width tip and tail and a third with a narrow shovel. Now imagine all these skis are flat on the snow and pointing down the fall line. If each ski is tilted onto its edge, can you see how the ski with the wider shovel is immediately more **advanced** in the turn simply by its shape?

Skis, therefore, have a wider shovel than tail to help start the new turn.

NERVOUS SKIS

A ski that has too much taper angle and sidecut can be nervous and tends to turn too easily. A nervous ski feels unstable when trying to ski in a straight line.

EDGE HOLD

Skis with too much taper angle have poorer **edge hold** (grip), because the rear of the ski is more prone to skidding across the snow. Can you visualise this from the diagrams?

SKIING IN SOFT SNOW

A wide shovel (due to taper angle) enables a ski to float through soft snow, rather than sink. This makes skiing in soft snow easier.

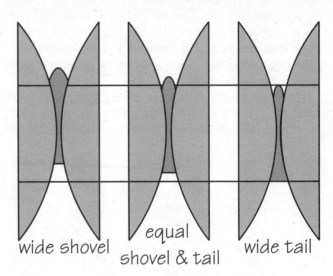

wide shovel

equal shovel & tail

wide tail

TAPER ANGLE GIVES LESS DRAG

Taper angle helps to reduce sidewall drag when travelling in a straight line, allowing your skis to travel **slightly** faster over the snow. The ski, being wider at the front, flattens the snow as it rides over it, clearing a path as it goes. This enables the sidewalls of the ski to pass through the snow with less drag. If the ski was narrower at the front, the sidewalls would rub against the snow, giving greater frictional resistance. Note that this effect is minimal.

Flex is the property a ski has to bend when a force is applied to it. Its role is twofold: to enable the ski to bend so that it can turn, yet be stiff enough to dampen vibration at speed in a straight line.

FLEX PATTERN

The flex pattern is a measure of a ski's stiffness along its length. Different flex patterns suit different conditions and uses of the ski.

In powder snow, it is advantageous to have a ski with a soft flex pattern so it can easily bend. Powder snow, being soft as feathers, makes it difficult to bend a stiff ski. Imagine how difficult it would be to bend a thick steel bar by hitting it against a feather pillow.

On ice, it is better to have a ski with a stiffer flex. Ice, being hard, needs a firm ski to help reduce vibration and give better edge hold.

When skiing through moguls (read pages 88-94 for information on moguls), a ski with a soft shovel and stiff tail is preferable. The soft shovel reduces the tendency for the ski to throw your weight back, by soaking up the undulating terrain. The stiff tail allows you to brake hard in the trough of the bump.

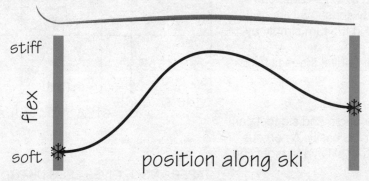

stiff

flex

soft

position along ski

PROFILE OF A SKI

Flex is controlled by the combination of materials used and the profile of the ski. The increase in thickness toward the centre makes the midsection of the ski more rigid. This is necessary to avoid excessive bending in the middle where your weight sits.

Ski designers create a profile that gives the right flex pattern for a particular type of ski.

COMPARING SKIS

The flex of different skis can be compared by bending them. Hold the tip of the ski with one hand, and secure the tail of the ski with your foot. With your free hand, press the centre of the ski.

Torsional Stiffness

MORE INFO

Torsional stiffness is the property a ski has to resist twisting, which occurs when your skis are tilted.

WASHING OUT
Tilting a moving ski onto its edge causes the tip and tail of the ski to twist. This reduces the grip of your edge and causes your skis to skid over the snow. This skidding due to your skis twisting is known as 'washing out'. Increasing your speed or the amount your skis are tilted increases the degree of twisting.

Washing out is most noticeable when skiing on hard icy surfaces, where any reduction in edge grip is easily felt.

AMOUNT OF TORSIONAL STIFFNESS
Skis with less torsional stiffness are less likely to catch an edge and are generally more forgiving to ski. This makes them more suited to beginner and intermediate skiers. Skis with greater torsional stiffness, though less forgiving, are preferred by advanced and expert skiers because they need a ski that does not twist at higher speeds and under aggressive use.

test torsional stiffness by twisting whole length of ski

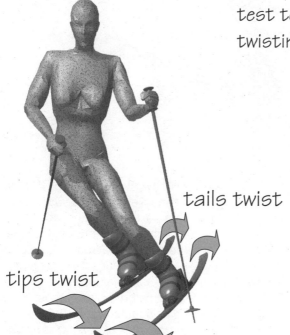

tails twist

tips twist

COMPARING TORSIONAL STIFFNESS
Torsional stiffness can be felt by supporting the tail of the ski between your feet and twisting the shovel with your hands. If another person is available, hold the ski horizontally and at opposite ends. One person twists the ski while the other holds it still.

Note that both these testing methods are not a true representation of what is happening on the snow because, when skiing, the tip and tail twist in the **same** direction from the centre of the ski.

Swing Weight

Swing weight relates to the **inertial moment** of the ski. Inertial moment is much more easily felt than described, but can be thought of as the rotational weight of the ski. In general terms, the swing weight reflects the ski's weight. The heavier the ski, the greater the swing weight.

TO FEEL THE SWING WEIGHT

Hold the ski at its centre and rotate it to and fro through ninety degrees.

Each time you try to change the direction of the ski, you will feel an opposing force on your arm. The force you feel is the extent of swing weight.

By repeating the exercise with different skis, you can compare their swing weights. You will find that it takes more time and effort to stop swinging heavier skis and reverse their direction. It's quicker and easier to change the direction of lighter skis.

Note: To make a fair comparison, skis must be the same length and without bindings.

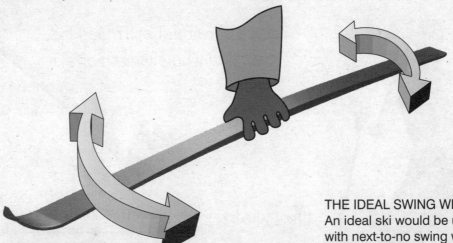

IMPORTANCE OF SWING WEIGHT

When using the parallel turn, you change your skis' direction of rotation from one turn to the next, particularly when making pivoted parallel turns (read pages 33-74 for information on parallel turns). Here, your skis rotate about their axes in a short space of time. A heavier ski is slower to come around into the new turn as it has greater swing weight. A lighter ski with less swing weight enables you to alternate turns more quickly and with less effort.

THE IDEAL SWING WEIGHT

An ideal ski would be ultra-light, with next-to-no swing weight. While as light a ski as possible is ideal, there is often a trade-off. A lighter construction usually means a weaker and less durable ski.

Technology is, as always, bringing us new materials, so maybe the future holds ultra-light, strong skis that last forever!

This chapter explains the parallel turn. This turn enables you to ski with your skis side by side, and makes skiing fun. The snowplough turn, while very practical, lacks grace and fluidity. In contrast, the parallel turn is dynamic, with a flowing motion that can make skiing exhilarating.

Imagine a smooth, fast run where the snow is just perfect. A controlled run through the bumps. A magic powder run through the lightest deepest snow you have ever seen. The parallel turn enables you to do it all.

NOTE: This chapter assumes you have read the previous chapter.

Introduction

The parallel turn is a complex technique with many variations, which are used to suit different snow conditions and terrain. This chapter explains the construction of the turn by first taking you through an overview of the two turning styles. It then looks at the individual body movements that make up each style. The following two chapters (Chapter 4 - SNOW TECHNIQUES and Chapter 5 - TERRAIN TECHNIQUES) explain how the parallel turn is used in different snow conditions and terrain.

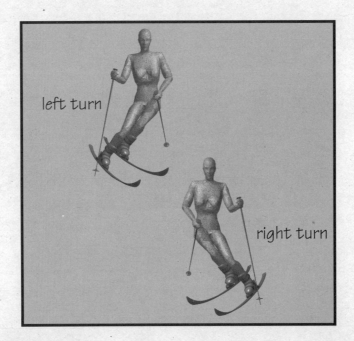

left turn

right turn

SNOWPLOUGH & PARALLEL TURN

When you make a snowplough turn, your legs are **apart**; one to the left side of your body and the other to the right. They are ready and waiting to turn you in either direction. To make turns down the fall line all you need do is alternate your weight from one leg to the other.

With the parallel turn there is the problem that both legs are angled to **one side** of your body. This means that to make a turn in the opposite direction, you have to alter your body's position in relation to your legs. This is what makes the turn more complex than the snowplough.

Types of Turns

The parallel turn can be skied in a vast range of styles, but all of these fit into one of two categories of turn. These are:

1. Pivoted/skidded turns
2. Carved turns

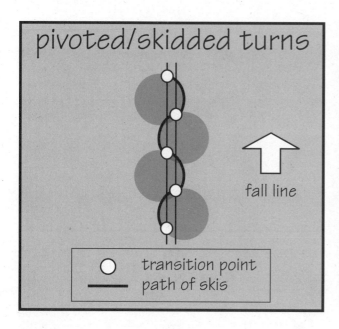

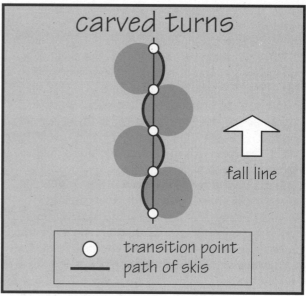

THE TRANSITION & TRANSITION POINT

The parallel turn is skied making **linked** turns; a left turn flows directly into a right turn and vice versa. The **transition** is the part of the turn where one turn finishes and the next turn in the opposite direction begins. The **transition point** is the moment in time where your skis are not edged (tilted), but flat against the snow because you are between turns.

  Notice how the transition points for pivoted turns follow two parallel rows of lines, but the transition points for carved turns follow a single line.

Pivoted/Skidded Turns

Pivoted/skidded turns are those where your skis are rotated during the transition. These turns are not always considered as elegant as carved turns, but are nonetheless the backbone of the parallel technique. They are the turns that work everywhere. Their excellent braking ability enables you to reduce speed to a manageable level. They are most useful for skiing difficult snow, moguls and moderate to steep slopes. The degree of pivoting can vary from **minimal** pivoting of a few degrees to **extensive** pivoting where your skis pivot past the fall line. Notice that when the pivoting is more extensive the transition points are near the extreme left and right of the turn.

REASONS FOR PIVOTING

There are four reasons for pivoting:

1. To help initiate turns: Pivoting your skis helps you initiate the next turn because it re-aligns your skis in the direction of the new turn.

2. To increase braking: Pivoting enables you to brake hard as you bring your skis across your old direction of travel. The hard braking that results from this causes your skis to skid, especially at the tails. Hence the name.

3. To make shorter pitch turns: Pivoting enables you to make shorter pitch turns than carving because you are not limited by the natural turning radius of the ski. Shorter pitched turns enable you to brake more frequently, so keep your speed down.

4. To prevent rapid acceleration: Pivoting your skis enables you to swing your unweighted skis through the fall line. This prevents you accelerating due to your skis pointing directly downhill while your weight is on them.

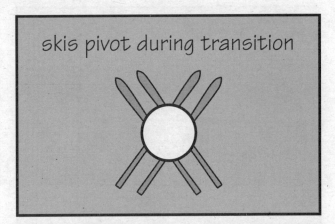

skis pivot during transition

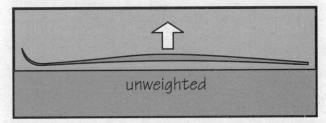

unweighted

THE TRANSITION

At the transition, your legs pass beneath your body, so your skis come onto their opposite edges to turn in the other direction.

Just before the transition, you take your weight **off** your skis, which allows you to pivot them. If your skis were under the pressure of your body's weight, pivoting would be impossible due to friction.

Pivoted/Skidded Turns

switching from a right to a left turn

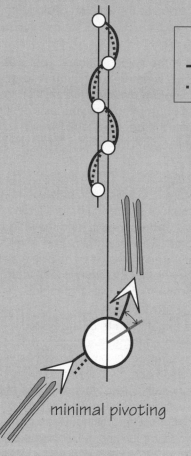

○ transition point
— path of skis
······· path of upper body

active edges

minimal pivoting

fall line

extensive pivoting
(skis brought through fall line)

Pivoted/Skidded Turns

MORE INFO

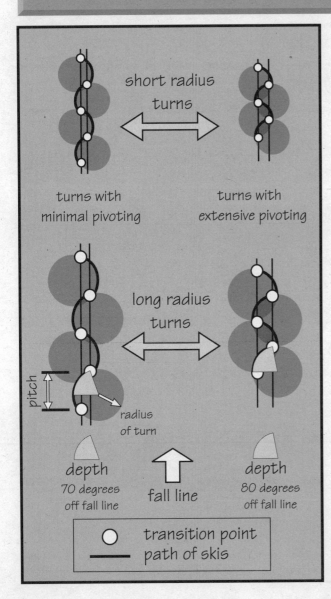

short radius turns

turns with minimal pivoting

turns with extensive pivoting

long radius turns

pitch

radius of turn

depth
70 degrees off fall line

fall line

depth
80 degrees off fall line

○ transition point
— path of skis

RADIUS OF TURN

The radius of a turn is controlled by how much your skis are **tilted**. The more you tilt your skis, the sharper they turn. The radius of a pivoted turn is hard to define due to the amount of skidding taking place.

DEPTH OF TURN

Depth of turn is the angle you steer your skis out of the fall line. This is determined by **how long** you ride your skis before making the transition into the next turn. The longer you ride your skis past the fall line, the greater the depth of turn. Pivoted turns tend to be of a similar depth, coming a long way across the fall line.

PITCH OF TURN

The pitch of turn is the distance between transition points. The pitch of pivoted turns is affected by the combination of **radius**, **depth**, and the amount your skis are **pivoted**. Shorter radius turns, shallower turns and extensively pivoted turns give a shorter pitch. Remember that the final pitch of a turn is due to the **combination** of all these variables.

DIRECTION & BRAKING

Pivoted turns enable you to change direction and brake hard. Pivoted turns (particularly extensively pivoted turns) offer better braking than carved turns as they compress and displace more snow because they bring your skis across your direction of travel.

The combination of deep and short radius turns gives the most effective braking. Deep turns bring your skis across the fall line, so slow you down. In contrast, shallow turns keep your skis closer to the fall line, where the braking power is less. Tight turns prevent you from gathering too much speed.

Pivoted/Skidded Turns

BODY MOVEMENTS THAT MAKE UP THE TURN

Pivoted turns are made up of five different body movements. For details of the movements see the next subsection of this chapter (pages 44-73).

pivoted turns

tilting ✓

pressing ✓

flexing & extending ✓

pivoting ✓

poling ✓

hip angulation ✓
knee angulation ✓
foot staggering ✓

weight forward or back ✓
weight one ski or both ✓

up unweighting ✓
terrain unweighting ✓
leg retraction ✓
body projection ✗

All body movements for the parallel technique are shown in this diagram. Movements with a tick are used for pivoted turns.

Carved Turns

Carved turns are turns where you don't pivot your skis at the transition and where there is minimal skidding taking place during the turn.

Carved turns are most useful when skiing fast, groomed runs. Carved turns compress and displace minimal snow, so give poor braking. This makes them less suitable on steep slopes where good braking is needed.

PERFECTLY CARVED TURNS ARE NOT POSSIBLE
Perfectly carved turns would cut clean arcs through the snow, but perfectly carved turns are not possible because your skis will always skid sideways to some degree, due to the snow collapsing under your weight. The plume of snow thrown up from the tail of your skis is evidence that this is happening. The closest you can get to a purely carved turn is when skiing on a very firm surface, almost ice, where the snow is soft enough for sharp edges to cut in to avoid skidding, but firm enough to support your weight.

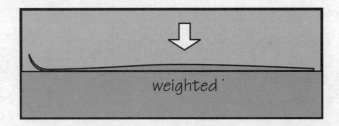

weighted

THE TRANSITION
At the transition, you rock your skis onto their opposite edges so you can turn in the other direction. To do this, you move your body across your skis and legs. With carved turns, you keep your weight **on** your skis so they **don't** pivot at the transition. This means that you flex and extend your legs differently from when making pivoted turns.

Carved Turns

switching from a right to a left turn

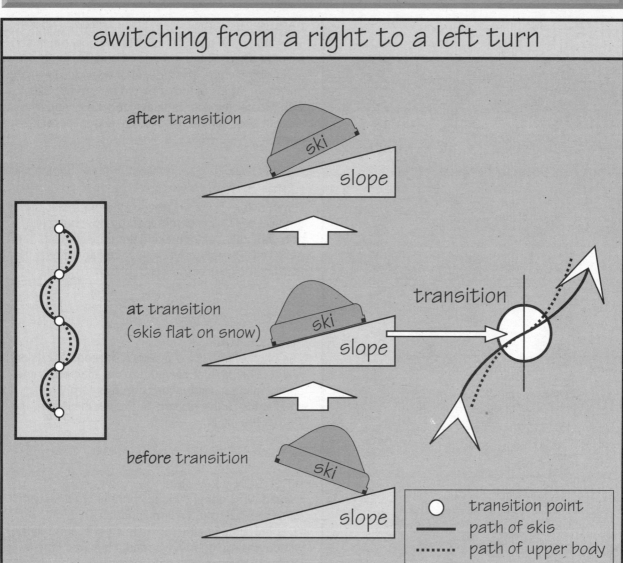

after transition

ski

slope

at transition
(skis flat on snow)

ski

slope

transition

before transition

ski

slope

○ transition point
— path of skis
.... path of upper body

Carved Turns

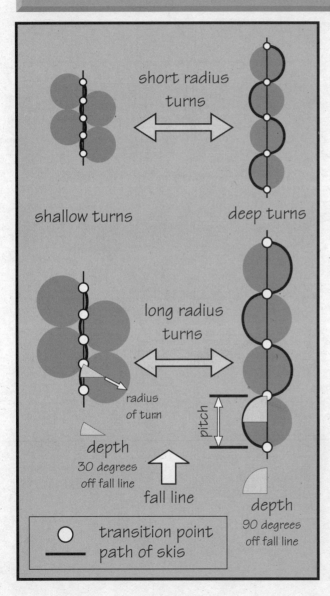

short radius turns

shallow turns

deep turns

long radius turns

radius of turn

pitch

depth
30 degrees
off fall line

fall line

depth
90 degrees
off fall line

○ transition point
— path of skis

RADIUS OF TURN

The radius of a turn is controlled by how much your skis are **tilted**. The more you tilt your skis, the sharper they turn. The sidecut of your skis limits the minimum radius of turn that can be carved. Skis with greater (smaller radius) sidecut e.g. super-sidecut skis, can be used to make smaller radius turns.

DEPTH OF TURN

Depth of turn is the angle you steer your skis out of the fall line. This is determined by **how long** you ride your skis before making the transition into the next turn. The longer your skis are carved past the fall line, the greater the depth of turn.

PITCH OF TURN

The pitch of turn is the distance between transition points. The pitch of carved turns is affected by the combination of **radius** and **depth** of turn. The smaller the radius and the shallower the depth, the shorter the pitch.

DIRECTION & BRAKING

Carved turns enable you to change direction with minimal braking (on a firm surface).

Carved turns enable racers to steer around gates without losing too much speed. However, time is lost by the increase in path length.

Carved Turns

MORE INFO

BODY MOVEMENTS THAT MAKE UP THE TURN

Carved turns are made up from three/four different body movements. Poling is often used when making carved turns, but carved turns can be made without using your poles. For details of the movements see the next subsection of this chapter (pages 44-73).

carved turns

tilting ✓

    hip angulation ✓
    knee angulation ✓
    foot staggering ✓

pressing ✓

    weight forward or back ✓
    weight one ski or both ✓

flexing & extending ✓

    up unweighting ✗
    terrain unweighting ✗
    leg retraction ✗
    body projection ✓

pivoting ✗

poling ✓ (optional)

All body movements for the parallel technique are shown in this diagram. Movements with a tick are used for carved turns.

Body Movements

The parallel technique consists of a combination of five different body movements:

1. Tilting: Tilting your skis enables them to flex and cut an arc through the snow and enables you to maintain balance. There are three leg movements that contribute to tilting.

2. Pressing: Distributing your body weight over your skis gives the pressure needed to flex them. There are two ways of doing this.

3. Flexing and extending: Flexing and extending your legs enables you to move your skis from one side of your body to the other. This is done by one of four methods. Three of these methods take your weight off your skis, enabling you to pivot them.

4. Pivoting: Pivoting your skis enables you to make pivoted turns.

5. Poling: Poling is necessary for pivoted turns and optional for carved turns. Poling also gives your skiing rhythm.

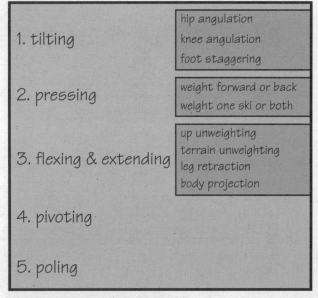

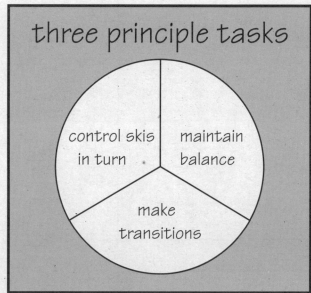

THREE PRINCIPLE TASKS

The body movements that make up the parallel technique enable you to:

1. Control your skis in the turn.

2. Maintain balance.

3. Make transitions from one turn to the next.

Tilting

There are three separate leg movements involved in tilting your skis. These are:
1. **Hip angulation**
2. **Knee angulation**
3. **Foot staggering**

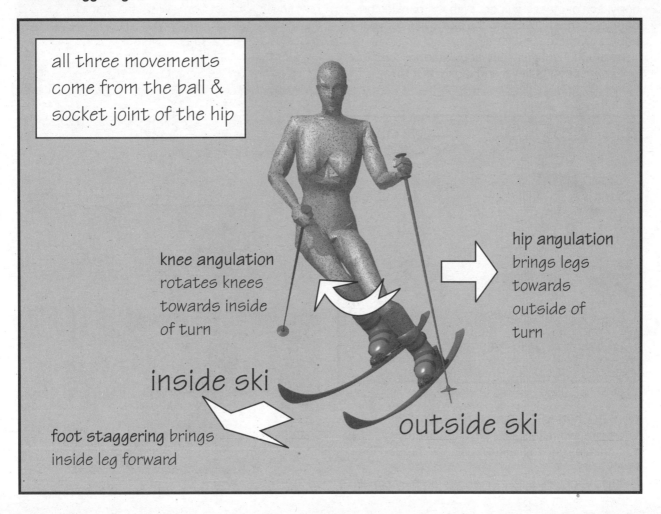

all three movements come from the ball & socket joint of the hip

knee angulation rotates knees towards inside of turn

hip angulation brings legs towards outside of turn

inside ski

outside ski

foot staggering brings inside leg forward

Hip Angulation

Hip angulation is the angling of your legs from the hip joint. This moves your feet to the side of your body. With the snowplough turn, both legs are angulated from the hip to **opposite** sides of your body, so your feet are apart. With the parallel turn, both legs are angulated to the **same** side of your body, so your feet are together.

The amount your legs are angulated will vary to suit your speed of travel and radius of turn.

TRY NOW

To simulate hip angulation:
1. With your ski boots on, stand in a sturdy doorway that is about 75 centimetres wide.
2. Position your body along one edge of the door frame.
3. Move your feet over to the opposite side of the doorway.

YOU ARE NOW USING HIP ANGULATION

When skiing, centripetal force supports your weight, rather than the door frame.

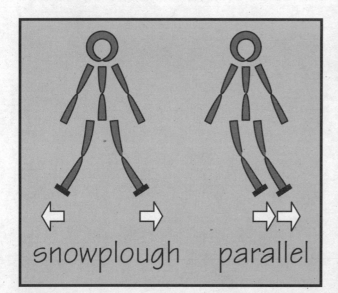

snowplough   parallel

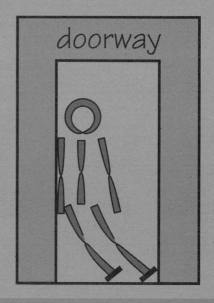

doorway

WHY DO YOU NEED TO HIP ANGULATE?
There are two reasons for hip angulation:
1. It enables you to maintain balance through the turn.
2. It tilts your skis onto their edges, so they can flex.

Hip Angulation

REASON 1.....Maintaining balance

HIP ANGULATION & BALANCE
Moving both feet to one side of the body may look unbalanced. However, when in motion and making a turn, a sideways force acts on you. The force would topple you over if you did not angulate your legs to compensate. The force is called **centripetal force** and is present when rotary motion takes place i.e. when turning.

BALANCE & CENTRIPETAL FORCE
Centripetal force varies with your **speed** and **radius** of turn. If you are skiing at a certain speed and make a particular radius turn, you will feel a corresponding sideways force.
  If you **double** your speed you will **quadruple** the centripetal force.
  If you **halve** the radius of turn, you will **double** the force.
  The magnitude of the centripetal force determines how much you need to angulate to stay in balance. The greater the force, the more you need to angulate.
  When you turn, you experience the combination of centripetal force and gravity, which appear to you as one force.

BALANCE IN OTHER SPORTS
Mountain bikers, cyclists and motorcyclists lean their whole body when turning. This enables them to maintain balance with centripetal force and gravity.

BALANCE IN SKIING
While cyclists angulate their whole body to maintain balance, skiers only angulate their legs for the majority of turns. The exception to this is for **banked** turns where the upper body is tilted as well. Banked turns are used when making high-speed carved turns (where additional angulation is needed for balance) or when skiing gunbarrels (where the whole body is tilted for balance and for fun).

REASON 2.....To tilt your skis

HIP ANGULATION TO TILT YOUR SKIS
Hip angulation causes your skis to tilt onto their
edges, enabling the sidecut of the ski to work. This
causes your skis to bend so they can cut an arc
through the snow.

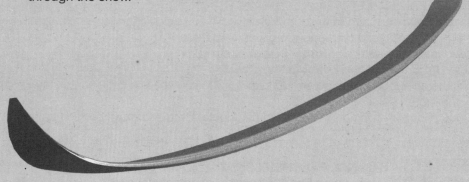

tilt

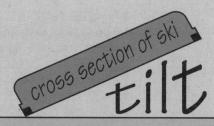

cross section of ski

tilt

snow

Knee Angulation

In the snowplough turn, knee angulation positions the tips of your skis together and the tails apart. With the parallel turn, both knees move in the **same** direction, towards the inside of the turn.

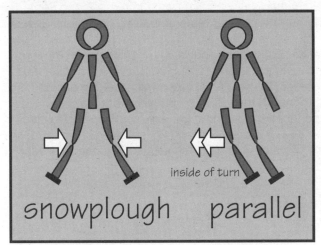

inside of turn

snowplough   parallel

WHAT HAPPENS DURING KNEE ANGULATION?

Knee angulation appears and feels like a sideways movement of the knee, but what may be surprising about the movement is that it causes a rotation of the leg. When you move your knee sideways your whole leg, including your foot, rotates from the **hip joint**. Note that your legs must be bent at the knees and ankles to allow this. If your legs are straight, they cannot rotate freely.

WHY DO YOU NEED TO KNEE ANGULATE?

The reason for knee angulation is to enable you to steer your skis in a turn by fine tuning the amount they are tilted. This particularly helps the initiation of turns.

TRY NOW

To simulate knee angulation:
With your ski boots on, stand with your feet hip-width apart and move your knees left, right, left, right.
 Notice how the soles of your ski boots tilt as you do so.

YOU ARE NOW USING KNEE ANGULATION

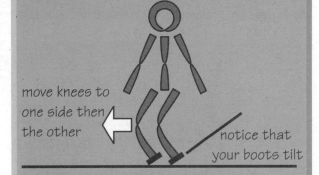

move knees to one side then the other

notice that your boots tilt

NOTE

This exercise also demonstrates how you can vary the tilt of your skis by moving your knees, without greatly affecting your balance. This is because your feet remain under your body. As you do the exercise you can maintain your balance, unlike the hip angulation exercise where you need to support your weight against a door frame.

Knee Angulation

REASON FOR KNEE ANGULATION.....To steer your skis

KNEE ANGULATION TO STEER YOUR SKIS
Think of your knees as the tools for steering your skis. Point them left when you want to turn left and right when want to turn right (if you remember only one thing from this chapter remember this). Using your knees in this way also helps you to initiate your turns.

Knee angulation is used in conjunction with hip angulation. Both cause your skis to tilt, but during the turn only hip angulation enables you to maintain balance with centripetal force. For a turn of a given radius and speed, hip angulation controls your balance and gives some tilt to your skis. Meanwhile, knee angulation enables you to **fine-tune** the amount your skis are tilted to **match** the radius of turn you want to make, without upsetting your balance. Both are adjusted independently throughout the turn, enabling you to steer your skis.

Note: less knee angulation is needed with super sidecut skis for a turn of given radius and speed because they turn sharper than conventional skis, for a given amount of tilt.

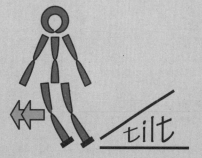

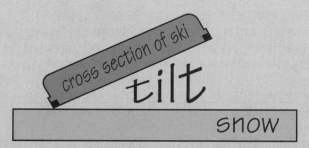

Foot Staggering

MORE INFO

Foot staggering is the positioning of your inside leg forward of your outside leg during each turn. The amount of foot staggering increases with speed and the steepness of slope.

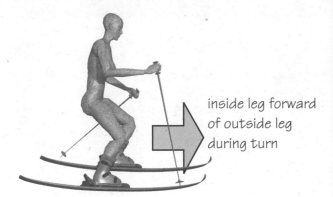

inside leg forward
of outside leg
during turn

WHY DO YOU NEED TO FOOT STAGGER?

There are two reasons for foot staggering, and three additional benefits it gives:

Reasons

Both of these reasons are due to ankle movement being limited by ski boots.

1. Foot staggering is needed so you can bend your inside leg more than your outside leg in a turn.
2. Foot staggering is needed so you can put more of your weight onto your outside ski in a turn.

Benefits

1. Facilitates knee angulation of the outside leg in the turn.
2. Helps to reduce the likelihood of ski tips crossing.
3. Aids fore and aft balance.

TRY NOW

To simulate ski staggering:
1. With your ski boots on, stand in a sturdy doorway that is about 75 centimetres wide.
2. Position your body along one edge of the door frame.
3. Move your feet over to the opposite side of the doorway.
4. Move the leg that represents the inside leg of the turn forward by half a boot length.

YOU ARE NOW USING FOOT STAGGERING

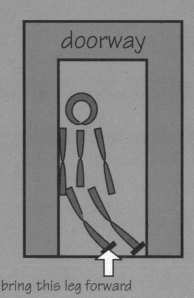

doorway

bring this leg forward

Foot Staggering

MORE INFO

REASON 1.....So your legs can bend by different amounts

WHY DO YOU NEED TO BEND YOUR LEGS BY DIFFERENT AMOUNTS?

Before looking at why foot staggering is necessary, it is helpful to understand why your inside leg has to be bent more than your outside leg in a turn. It is because the distance from your hip joint to the inside leg's ski is **shorter** than the distance from the hip joint to the outside leg's ski. There are three things that contribute to this:

1. The inside leg may have less hip angulation than the outside leg, causing your feet to be more than hip-width apart. This is so when skiing fast, or on an icy surface (see page 80).

2. Your pelvis may be tilted by varying amounts. The faster you ski, the more your pelvis tilts in the turn.

3. The angle of slope causes your skis to sit at different heights, the steeper the slope, the greater the height difference. Deeper turns which bring your skis further across the slope make the affect of slope angle more pronounced.

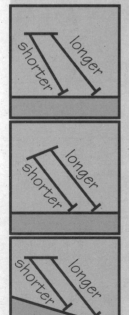

inside leg has less hip angulation

pelvis tilts

slope angle

combination of all three

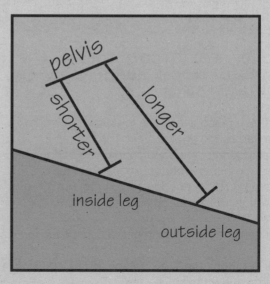

Foot Staggering

REASON 1.....continued

FOOT STAGGERING TO BEND INSIDE LEG
When wearing normal footwear, it is simple to stand with one leg bent more than the other, with your feet alongside each other. This is because your legs can bend at all three joints i.e. at the **hip**, **knee** and **ankle**.

When wearing ski boots ankle movement is restricted. To stand with one leg bent more than the other in ski boots means that movement has to come from the **hip** and **knee** joints. Bending from only two joints brings the foot forward, causing your feet to be staggered.

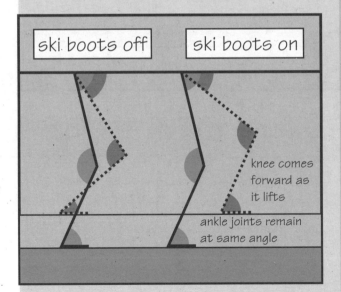

ski boots off ski boots on

knee comes forward as it lifts

ankle joints remain at same angle

TRY NOW

To help understand the relationship between boot flex and foot staggering:

1. Find a single step or use the lowest stair of a staircase.
2. Stand side-on to step, barefoot or in shoes
3. Place one foot on the step, while keeping your feet alongside each other.
 Notice how the higher leg is bent more at the hip, knee and ankle joints.

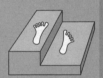

4. Repeat exercise wearing ski boots that are **fully buckled up**.
 Notice how it feels awkward to stand with both feet side by side.

5. Position your higher leg forward (this is the inside leg when making a parallel turn).
 Notice how this feels more natural.
 Notice how the hip and knee joints of the higher leg are bent more than those of the lower leg, whilst both ankle joints maintain the same angle, due to the ski boot.

Foot Staggering

REASON 2.....So you can weight your outside ski only

TWO POINTS RELATING TO WEIGHT DISTRIBUTION
The details of weight distribution are looked at later in this chapter (see pages 57-64).
1. When skiing, your shins press against the tongues of your boots, causing the cuffs to flex forward. In the turn, the cuffs flex further as centripetal force causes your legs to push harder against them.
2. When turning, your weight can be supported by **both** your legs, but often you will support your weight with just your **outside** leg.

BOTH LEGS WEIGHTED
If you make a turn with your weight forward and on both skis, the cuffs of both boots will flex.

OUTSIDE LEG WEIGHTED
If you turn with your weight forward and with your weight on the outside ski, that boot cuff will flex, causing the pelvis to lower slightly. The inside leg cannot move in the same way because there is **no pressure** being applied to the cuff of that boot. This means that movement has to come instead from the hip and knee joints causing the inside foot to move forward which increases foot staggering.

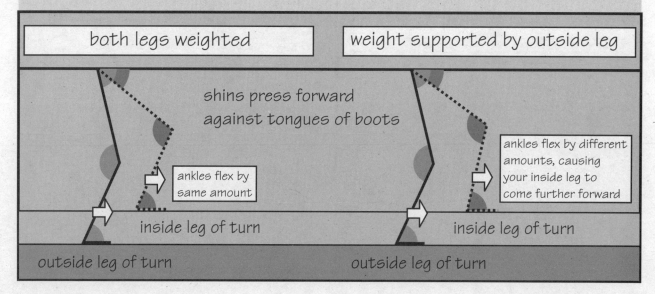

REASON 2.....continued

TRY NOW

To help understand how your weight distribution affects foot staggering:

1. With your ski boots on, stand with your feet side-by-side on a level surface. Press your shins into the fronts of your boots.
  Notice how both boots flex evenly under the load.

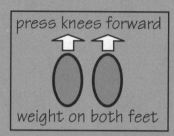

press knees forward

weight on both feet

2. Now put all your weight on one foot, pressing that shin into the front of the boot.
  Notice how your weighted boot flexes more under the extra load.

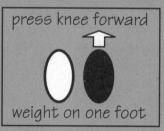

press knee forward

weight on one foot

3. Now move your unweighted foot forward. Then press the shin of your weighted foot into the front of the boot.
  Notice how much your weighted boot now flexes. Moving the unweighted leg forward out of the way has made it easier to flex your weighted boot.

press knee forward

weight on one foot

Foot Staggering

BENEFIT 1.....Facilitates Knee Angulation

FOOT STAGGERING & KNEE ANGULATION
Foot staggering moves the inside leg forward. This allows the outside leg to come in behind the inside leg when knee angulating in the turn. This avoids the inside leg obstructing the movement of the outside leg.

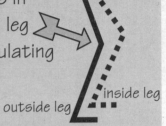

rear knee tucks in behind forward leg when knee angulating

outside leg

inside leg

BENEFIT 2.....Reducing Tip Crossing

FOOT STAGGERING & TIP CROSSING
Foot staggering helps to reduce tip crossing, which is a common problem when learning the parallel turn. Having your inside ski forward allows the tip of the outside ski to act as a **guard** preventing your inside ski sliding over it.

tip of outside ski acts as a guard to reduce tip crossing

BENEFIT 3.....Aiding Fore & Aft Balance

FOOT STAGGERING & BALANCE
Staggering your legs adds to your fore and aft stability. This gives you more control over balance. Can you imagine how you are more stable when standing with one leg forward, rather than with both legs side by side?

increased fore and aft stability

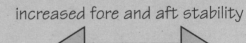

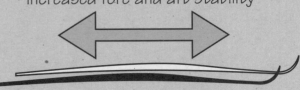

Pressing

Your weight has to press onto your skis to flex them. There are several ways you can distribute your weight onto your skis. These are:
1. **Weight forward or back**
2. **Weight one ski or both**

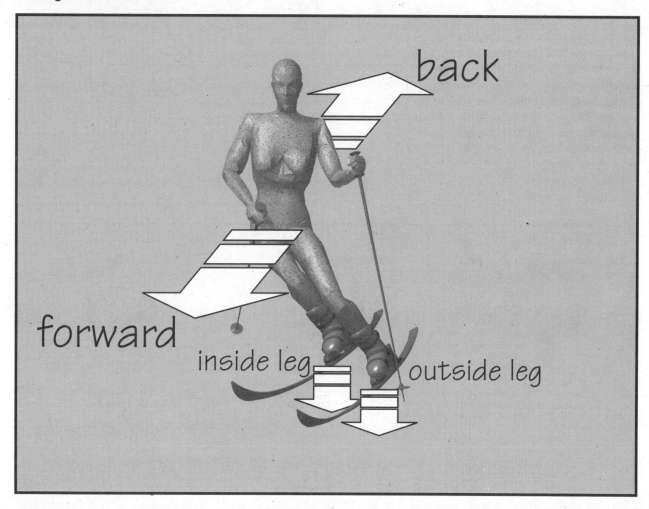

When skiing you must adjust your weight forward or backward over your skis. One reason for this is to stay in balance, another reason is because you must use your weight as a tool to control the shape of your skis.

CENTRE OF GRAVITY

Your centre of gravity is the point at the centre of your mass. To illustrate centre of gravity you may find it helpful to consider the centre of mass of other objects.

Your weight is **central** over your skis when your centre of gravity is directly over the **middle** of your ski boot soles (see drawing below).

Remember that your centre of gravity will change when you change your body position (shape).

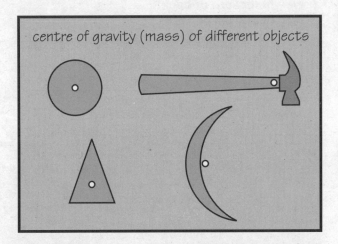

centre of gravity (mass) of different objects

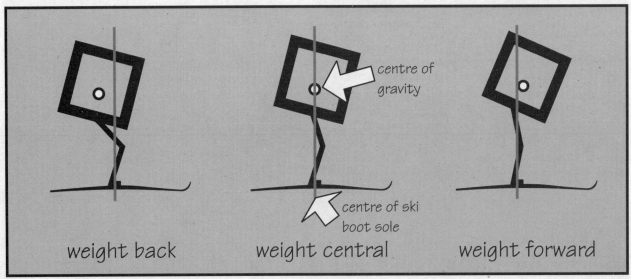

centre of gravity

centre of ski boot sole

weight back   weight central   weight forward

Weight Forward or Back

WHERE SHOULD YOUR WEIGHT BE?

For most conditions, you should keep your centre of gravity forward of centre. Keeping your weight forward promotes more bending in the front half of your skis, allowing them to cut a smooth arc through the snow to give a stable turn. In contrast, leaning back takes the pressure off the front of your skis, giving the front of the skis minimal flex. This hinders your turning and causes you to skate around on the tails of your skis with little control.

When turning, positioning your weight centrally is academic, as skiing over uneven terrain at speed means that you are constantly making adjustments to your balance. Your weight is therefore forward where it should be, or it is back and you are in the process of trying to move it forward again.

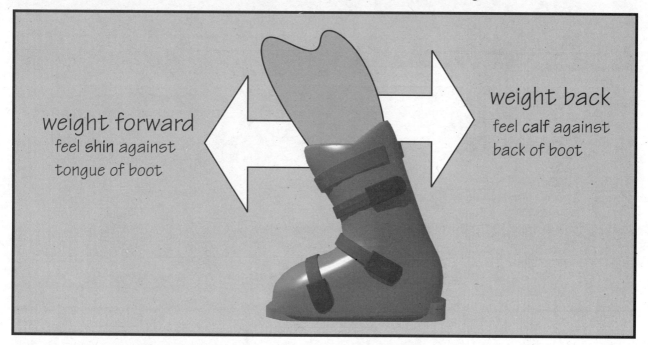

weight forward
feel shin against
tongue of boot

weight back
feel calf against
back of boot

FEEL WHERE YOUR WEIGHT IS

When you ski you can feel where your weight is. If your weight is forward, you will feel your shins pressing against the tongues of your ski boots. If your weight is back, you will feel your calves pressing against the back of your boots.

TRY NOW

To simulate weight distribution forward & back:

1. Put on a ski boot and ski.

2. Position the ski tip against a wall (you may want to protect the wall to avoid marking it).

3. Try to move your shin towards the toe piece of your ski binding, so your shin presses against the tongue of your boot. As you do this the ski will bend.

 Notice that it is the front half of the ski that is flexing.

YOU NOW HAVE YOUR WEIGHT FORWARD ON THE SKI

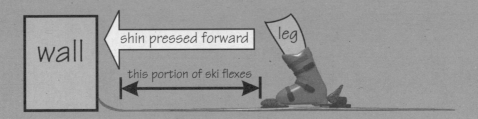

wall

shin pressed forward

leg

this portion of ski flexes

4. Now position the tail of your ski against the wall.

5. Press your calf against the back of the boot.

 Notice that it is the rear half of the ski that is flexing.

YOU NOW HAVE YOUR WEIGHT BACK ON THE SKI

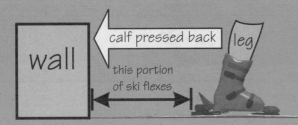

wall

calf pressed back

leg

this portion
of ski flexes

Weight Forward or Back

CONTROLLING WEIGHT POSITION

The parallel turn is dynamic. You continually need to make adjustments to maintain balance and to keep your weight forward on your skis. Learning to anticipate helps you to keep one step ahead of the terrain. Keeping your weight forward takes some effort; it is much easier to let your weight drop back. Boots with more forward lean (see page 116 for information on forward lean) enable you to position your weight further forward, which is helpful.

When standing in shoes you can bend your knees and still stand with your weight between the balls of your feet and your heels. You can do this because your ankle and hip joints bend with your knees. When wearing ski boots, ankle movement is restricted, so bending your knees forces your weight back. To compensate for this you have to bring your upper body forward when your legs flex. When turning you have to flex and extend your legs. Flexing and extending is covered later in this chapter (see pages 65-9).

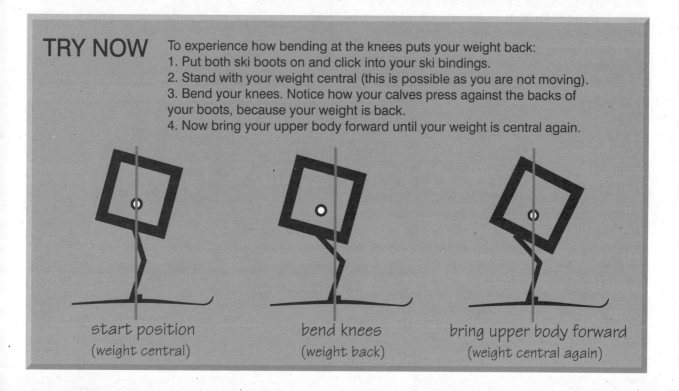

TRY NOW To experience how bending at the knees puts your weight back:
1. Put both ski boots on and click into your ski bindings.
2. Stand with your weight central (this is possible as you are not moving).
3. Bend your knees. Notice how your calves press against the backs of your boots, because your weight is back.
4. Now bring your upper body forward until your weight is central again.

start position
(weight central)

bend knees
(weight back)

bring upper body forward
(weight central again)

Weight Forward or Back

WEIGHT DISTRIBUTION & SLOPE ANGLE

Slope angle alters the position of your weight. On an inclined slope, you can position your weight further forward. The steeper the slope, the more your weight can come forward.

At the end of a turn, when you turn your skis out of the fall line and across the slope, they level out. The amount varies with depth of turn. The deeper the turn, the more they level out. This feels like your ski tips are lifting up, and your weight feels as if it is being pushed back.

It is helpful to increase pressure on the tail of your skis at the end of the turn, to prevent the tails skidding excessively. But if your weight is too far back, it can be hard to initiate the next turn.

Anticipating this change in angle with each turn can prevent you from being caught off guard. To compensate, bring your upper body forward.

weight moves forward
when skis point downhill

WEIGHT DISTRIBUTION & ACCELERATION

When your skis face down the fall line, it is possible to position your weight further forward on your skis. But when they **first** come around to pointing down the fall line, they accelerate. This feels like somebody pulling the rug from under your feet. Your skis take off down the slope, and your body is thrown backward.

To remedy this, anticipate the problem by moving your upper body forward, and thus your weight, forward.

if not corrected your body will be pushed back
onto the tails of your skis, when they accelerate

As you turn, you angulate your legs to maintain balance, so you do not topple over towards the outside of the turn. When angulating and resisting the centripetal force of the turn, you will find that your outside leg is in the stronger position to support you. Your outside leg will naturally take most of your weight.

TRY NOW

To simulate resisting centripetal force.

Method 1.
1. Get a friend to hold your hand and pull you sideways (towards the outside of the turn). This simulates centripetal force.
  As you try to stay in balance notice how most of your weight is on the leg closest to the person pulling you (the outside leg of the turn).

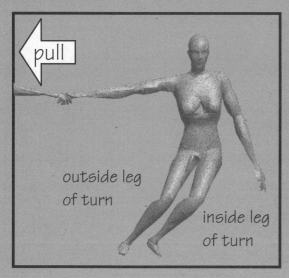

pull

outside leg
of turn

inside leg
of turn

Method 2.
1. Stand in a doorway, with your legs angulated to the side.
2. Try to push against the door frame that you are leaning against. First use your leg that represents the inside leg, then the leg that represents the outside leg.
  Notice how you can push harder with the outside leg.

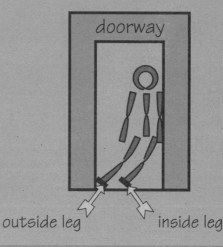

doorway

outside leg   inside leg

WEIGHT EACH SKI TO SUIT THE CONDITIONS

As you ski, you choose how much weight you apply to each ski to suit the snow conditions. On firm snow you naturally support most of your weight on the outside ski. In deep snow you need to weight your skis more evenly, so that one ski does not sink deeper into the soft snow than the other, which will throw you off balance (read pages 82-5 for details).

TIGHTENING THE TURN

By transferring all your weight to one ski (the outside ski), it will flex more under the load, thus tightening the turn.

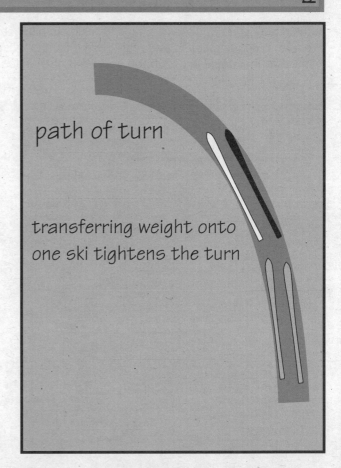

path of turn

transferring weight onto one ski tightens the turn

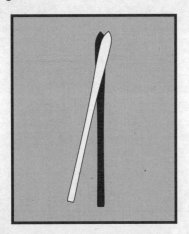

CROSSED SKIS

Taking the pressure off your inside ski creates the situation where the outside ski is under pressure and following an arc, while the inside ski is not under pressure and therefore not following an arc. This combination tends to cause the unweighted ski to waver in the snow and cross over your outside ski.

In the early days of learning the parallel turn, when tip crossing can often happen, keep weight on the inside ski to help it track alongside the outside ski.

As experience is gained you can experiment by putting more weight on the outside ski.

Flexing & Extending

Flexing and extending are necessary to make pivoted and carved turns. Flexing and extending facilitate the transition between turns, where your legs come under your body and then re-angulate to start the new turn. For pivoted turns, flexing and extending must also take your weight off your skis to eliminate the friction between your skis and the snow, so that your skis can pivot freely.

There are four methods of flexing and extending:

1. **Up unweighting**
2. **Terrain unweighting**
3. **Leg retraction**
4. **Body projection**

CHOOSING A METHOD

The method of flexing and extending dictates the type of turn you make:

For **pivoted** turns there are three choices. The one you choose depends on the type of terrain that you are skiing.

Up unweighting... For even angled slopes.
Terrain unweighting... For roll overs.
Leg retraction... For undulating terrain such as moguls.

For **carved** turns, there is only one choice... **Body projection**.

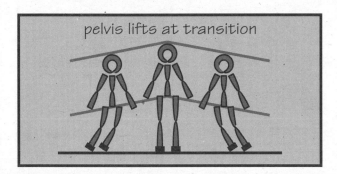

pelvis lifts at transition

RAISING YOUR PELVIS

Imagine cycling down the road, making turns left and right, one flowing into the next. With each turn your body and bike lean over to maintain balance with centripetal force and gravity. To make a turn in the opposite direction, your bike saddle has to rise **up and over**, so that you can turn the other way.

When turning on skis, your legs are angulated from the hip outward to the side of your body. This lowers your pelvis toward the snow just as the bike seat moves closer to the road when turning. To turn the other way, your pelvis has to rise like the bike seat. All four flexing and extending techniques raise your pelvis in relation to the snow surface, but do so in different ways. Up unweighting and body projecting rely on your legs lifting your body, while terrain unweighting and leg retraction instead rely (at least in part) on the ground dropping away.

If your pelvis did not rise, your legs would have to bend excessively as they pass under your body. This would throw your weight back onto the tails of your skis, making them difficult to control.

WEIGHT ON OR OFF SKIS

When making pivoted turns, up unweighting, terrain unweighting and leg retraction **remove** your weight from your skis so you can pivot them.

When carving using body projection, your weight remains **on** your skis as no pivoting takes place.

Up Unweighting

Up unweighting is used for **pivoted** turns on **even-angled** terrain. It is the most common unweighting method used.

HOW IT WORKS
Up unweighting is a similar motion to jumping, but you keep your skis in contact with the snow. Your legs flex and then extend to take your weight off your ski bases. This enables you to re-angulate your legs for the next turn and pivot your skis freely. Note: flexing your legs is automatically helped by the centripetal force pressing on your body. To extend your legs, you have to push against your skis, increasing the load on them. It is not until after the up unweighting motion is complete that your weight comes off the snow.

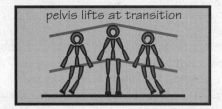

pelvis lifts at transition

TECHNIQUE
Before the transition point, you flex your legs so they can then extend and raise your body upward. This lifts your pelvis away from the snow. As your pelvis rises, your legs come under your body.

At the transition point, your legs are underneath you and your weight is off your skis, allowing you to pivot them.

After the transition point, begin to angulate your legs to make the new turn, putting your skis onto their opposite edges.

During the transition you pivot your skis.

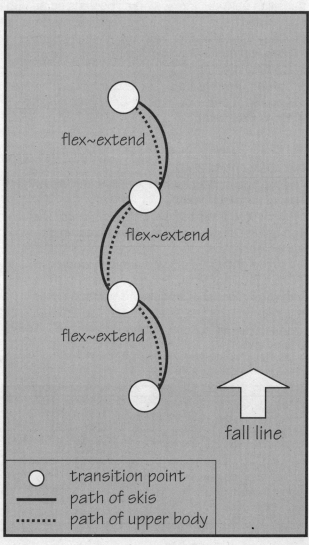

flex~extend

flex~extend

flex~extend

fall line

○ transition point
— path of skis
.... path of upper body

Terrain unweighting is used for **pivoted** turns when the terrain steepens up beneath you at a **roll over**. It is particularly helpful when skiing through difficult deep snow because it makes the new turn easier to initiate. It is delightful to use on a powder day, gliding over the crest of a roll and pivoting in the air.

HOW IT WORKS

As the ground drops away at a roll over, your weight automatically comes off the bases of your skis, making up unweighting unnecessary. Your legs can then move to the opposite side of your body and your skis can pivot freely as they do so.

TECHNIQUE

As you terrain unweight you can still make the flexing and extending motions that you would when up unweighting, but to a much lesser degree. This keeps your rhythm going. Also maintain your pole plant.

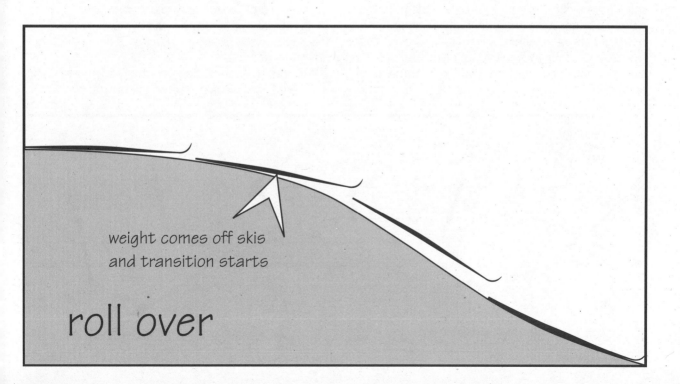

weight comes off skis
and transition starts

roll over

Leg Retraction

Leg retraction is used for **pivoted** turns when a **dip precedes a roll over** in the terrain, or when skiing the **rut line** through a mogul field, where it is the only technique that works effectively (for details of mogul skiing read page 88-94).

dip

roll over

HOW IT WORKS

To pivot your skis, you need to unweight them. But when a dip in the terrain precedes a roll over, it is very easy to be projected right off the snow and up into the air. Leg retraction enables you to **soak up** the terrain by flexing your legs before the roll over, so you can keep the amount of unweighting to a manageable level. After the lip of the roll over where the ground drops away, you can pivot your skis unhindered and re-angulate your legs for the next turn.

TECHNIQUE

1. As you ski up the ramp towards the roll over, retract your legs by flexing them to soak up the rise in terrain. At the same time vary your hip angulation to bring your legs under your body.
2. At the lip of the roll over, plant your pole.
3. Immediately after the lip pivot your skis. Then begin to extend your legs again and angulate them for the next turn.

With your legs extended you are ready for the next unweighting by whichever technique you choose.

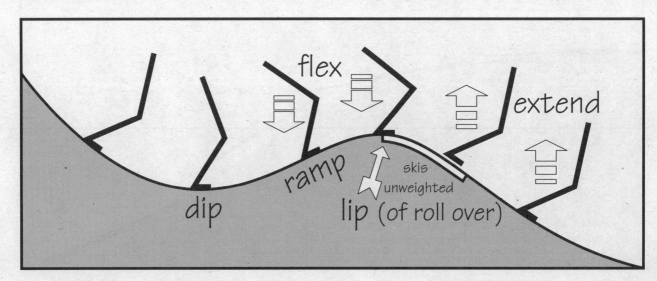

flex

extend

dip

ramp

skis unweighted

lip (of roll over)

Body Projection

MORE INFO

When making **carved** turns, use body projection as the flexing extending method.

HOW IT WORKS

The idea with body projection is to keep your weight on your skis (so they don't pivot) and project your body across them, so that your skis **roll** onto their opposite edges, giving a carved turn.

Your pelvis is highest above the snow at the transition point. This may seem surprising as your legs are most flexed at this position. But because your legs are directly under your body (no leg angulation), at the transition your upper body is lifted.

Snowboarders illustrate the idea of body projection better than skiers as their movements (although different in detail) are more obvious. Watch how snowboarders ride their boards on one edge, then flip their body over to the other side of the board, putting the board onto its opposite edge.

pelvis lifts at transition

TECHNIQUE

Before the transition point, flex your legs and move your body over your skis, then extend your legs as you angulate them for the new turn. This should be one flowing motion.

You may find it helpful to think of projecting your body over your skis as you make the transition rather than thinking of bringing your legs under your body.

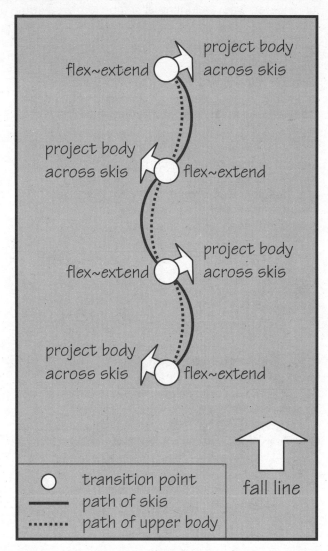

project body across skis
flex~extend

project body across skis
flex~extend

project body across skis
flex~extend

project body across skis
flex~extend

fall line

○ transition point
── path of skis
...... path of upper body

When making **pivoted** parallel turns, you have to pivot your skis during the transition. For your skis to rotate unhindered, your weight must first be removed from your skis by unweighting them using flexing and extending.

COUNTER ROTATION
Counter rotation enables you to pivot your skis gracefully without resorting to throwing your whole body around in an energetic lunge. This is how it works:
1. During the turn, remain facing down the fall line, while your legs follow the turn and come across the slope. This winds your body up like a spring.
2. When your weight comes off your skis using flexing and extending, untwist your body (unwind the spring) so that your skis pivot.

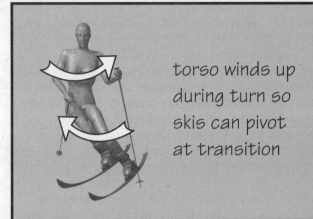

torso winds up during turn so skis can pivot at transition

TRY NOW
To simulate counter-rotation:

1. Stand on the balls of your feet.
2. Flex your legs
3. Move your knees to one side of your body until your body rotates almost 90 degrees.
4. Try this again but this time twist your upper body in the opposite direction, so it does **not** rotate with your legs. You are now wound up like a spring.
5. Jump up as in up unweighting and unwind the spring so your feet pivot.

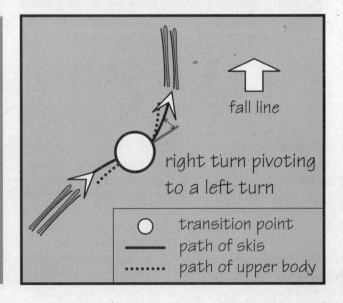

fall line

right turn pivoting to a left turn

○ transition point
— path of skis
······ path of upper body

Pivoting

DIRECTION OF UPPER BODY

Keeping your upper body (head, shoulders, and chest) **continually** facing down the fall line is vital when making pivoted parallel turns. This is in contrast to snowplough turns and carved parallel turns where your upper body rotates with each turn to face in the same direction as your skis.

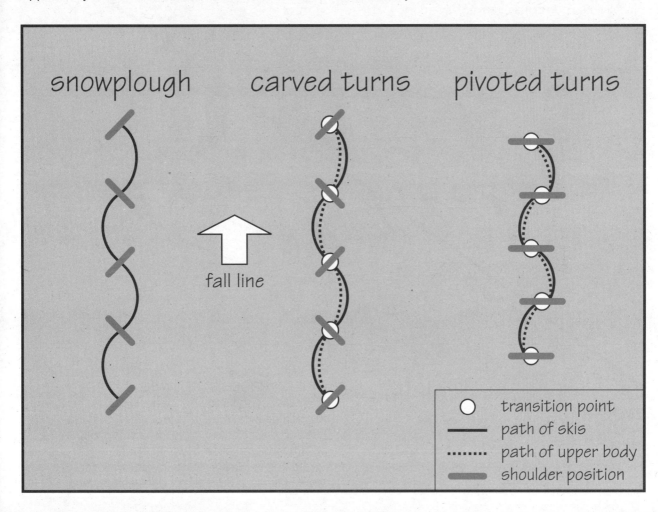

snowplough   carved turns   pivoted turns

fall line

○ transition point
— path of skis
⋯⋯ path of upper body
▬ shoulder position

Pivoting

LOOKING FORWARD AS YOU SKI

One way to help keep your upper body facing down the fall line when making pivoted turns is to pick a stationary object ahead of you that is further down the fall line. Look at it as you ski toward it.

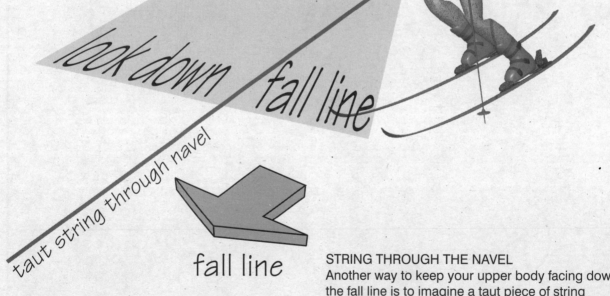

look down

fall line

taut string through navel

fall line

STRING THROUGH THE NAVEL

Another way to keep your upper body facing down the fall line is to imagine a taut piece of string passing through your navel. The string follows the fall line and you slide down it.

Note that in reality your body does not follow a straight line but drifts left or right with each turn.

Poling

Poling is necessary for **pivoted** turns. For **carved** turns, poles take a lesser role and are not always planted.

POLING HELPS UP UNWEIGHTING
When making pivoted turns using up unweighting, use your pole to help lift your body upward.

POLING HELPS PIVOTING
When making pivoted turns, pole planting aids pivoting by giving you a reference point in firm contact with the ground. This helps you keep your upper body facing down the fall line as your lower body rotates, and aids balance.

POLING GIVES RHYTHM
A musician uses a metronome to keep in time; a dancer uses music; skiers use their poles. Poling synchronises all the movements that make up the turn, so they all happen at the right time. The rhythm that it gives enables you to make symmetrical left and right turns.

Poling alters the **frequency** of your turns. The faster you pole, the quicker you change from one turn to the next, and vice versa.

PLANTING & REMOVING YOUR POLE
Choosing when to plant your pole depends on which flexing extending technique you are using.

When **up unweighting**, plant your pole as you flex your legs.

When **terrain unweighting**, poling is the same as for up unweighting, as the up unweighting motion is still present.

When using **leg retraction**, plant your pole at the lip of the bump or roll over, just before you make the transition.

When using **body projection**, plant your pole at the transition point, just as you finish flexing and begin to extend.

For all techniques be sure not to leave your pole planted too long because your hand, arm and shoulder will be left behind, causing your upper body to rotate. This will make you veer off to the side instead of following the fall line. When skiing faster, plant your pole a little further forward to help avoid skiing too far past it before removing it.

Parallel Tips

Learning the parallel turn is like climbing a ladder; you progress one rung at a time. The first rung is to teach your body the basic movements. To make this easier, experiment in an environment where you feel comfortable, such as where you can easily ski with the snowplough technique.

 Once you have learnt the basic parallel movements, you are on your way up the ladder. Each subsequent rung will give you the ability to use the parallel technique in increasingly demanding situations.

WHICH TECHNIQUE FIRST

Pivoted turns using up unweighting as the flexing and extending technique are the first to learn.

 Carved turns come later, once you can handle greater speeds.

KEY POINTS TO LEARNING THE BASICS

Here are some key points to focus on:

1. Tilt your skis. Move your legs out from under your body and use your knees to steer your turns. Keep your inside leg forward.

2. Keep your weight forward.

3. Flex and extend your legs, so you can unweight your skis with up-unweighting.

4. Use your poles to help you up-unweight and give you rhythm.

5. Use counter rotation to help you pivot by keeping your upper body pointing down the fall line.

EQUIPMENT

Three common equipment problems are:

1. Skis too long and too stiff (read pages 110-1 & 113). A **short pair of parabolic skis** will make learning easier than using longer conventional skis. If you want to get better more quickly then this is the way to go. And it's probably more fun too.

2. Boots too upright and too stiff (read page 116-7).

3. Poles too long (read page 124).

 Remember to wax your skis to make turning easier (read pages 144-7 for information on waxing).

CATCH TWENTY-TWO

Parallel turns are dynamic. They need to be made with a certain amount of speed. The catch is that when first learning the technique it is hard to ski with enough speed to make them work and still be in control. Experiment with your speed when you feel that you are in a safe enough situation for yourself and other skiers around you. Remember speed helps.

LEARN BY WATCHING

Watching good skiers can be most helpful in learning what to do. When first looking at what is happening it may appear puzzling. You can see their movements, but can't make any sense of them. So much is happening in such a short space of time. I recommend understanding fully the five basic body movements. Then you will know what it is you are looking for. Try to focus on one thing at a time as you watch other skiers i.e. pivoting, poling.

‘the snow and terrain are our teachers’

How Snow Forms
Snow Conditions
    Skiing Firm Snow
    Skiing Ice
    Skiing Crust
    Skiing Soft Snow
    Skiing Spring Snow

This chapter explains how snow forms and how you use the parallel turn in different types of snow.

    Learning how to ski different types of snow makes skiing interesting and challenging.

NOTE: This chapter assumes you have read the previous two chapters.

Snow forms within clouds. Clouds consist of water vapour (water as a gas), tiny water droplets, ice crystals and a variety of microscopic particles such as dust. Some dust particles have a role in the formation of snow crystals.

water droplet   snow crystal

condensation nuclei

freezing nuclei

IMPORTANCE OF PARTICLES
The microscopic particles in clouds have two roles in snow formation:
1. Some particles act as **condensation nuclei**. These provide a surface for water vapour to condense onto causing tiny droplets to form. But some water molecules collide with each other to form droplets with no nuclei.
2. Others act as **freezing nuclei.** Droplets freeze between zero and minus forty degrees Celsius. Droplets with freezing nuclei tend to freeze at warmer temperatures than those without. Droplets that remain liquid below zero degrees Celsius are known as **supercooled water droplets**.

The same particle may act as a freezing and condensation nucleus.

CRYSTAL GROWTH
Frozen droplets continue to grow into snowflakes by:
Deposition: where additional free molecules of water vapour attach themselves, they create delicate snowflakes.
Riming: where supercooled water droplets collide with snowflakes, they freeze instantly and maintain their bead-like shape. If riming is excessive, a snowflake becomes completely coated with tiny beads of ice, turning it into graupel (a particular type of snow).
Aggregation: where collisions occur between ice crystals, they lock together. Some collisions and air turbulence may cause crystals to break apart. When this happens, the fragments develop into separate snowflakes.

All three methods of growth may occur simultaneously within a cloud.

Crystals that don't melt on the downward journey arrive on the ground as snowflakes.

NON-PRECIPITATED CRYSTALS
While most crystals form in clouds, some grow at ground level. **Hoarfrost** is a leaf-like (often beautiful) crystal formation that grows when the air cools (usually at night). **Rime** occurs when supercooled water droplets contact an object. This is often seen on the windward side of posts and fences, but can cover vast areas. It can grow more rapidly when it's windy because the wind delivers more droplets to the surface it is growing on.

Snow is an amazing medium, continually changing so that no two days are the same on any mountain. There are over seventy types of snow crystal and an infinite number of snow conditions. Each time we go skiing it gives us a new experience. On some days the snow is just perfect everywhere, but at other times it is marginal and the best snow takes some finding.

   Skiing in different snow conditions is demanding on technique. On some days the parallel turn is easy to use, but on others it is hard work to keep from falling. The variations in snow demand that you modify your technique to suit the conditions. While there are many snow conditions that you may come across, there are five broad situations that you can expect to experience.

These are:

1. Skiing firm snow
2. Skiing ice
3. Skiing crust
4. Skiing soft snow
5. Skiing spring snow

ANTICIPATION
Reading the snow in front of you enables you to anticipate your skis' behaviour, keeping you one step ahead.

Experience enables you to:
a) Observe the snow's surface for telltale signs of its type.
b) Get a feel for the snow conditions by listening to the sound of your skis and other people's in the snow.
c) Judge the conditions by watching other people ski.

> ‘reading the snow in front of you enables you to anticipate your skis' behaviour’

Skiing Firm Snow

MORE INFO

The firm snow technique enables you to ski a variety of snow types. Firm snow provides a stable surface to ski over, while being soft enough for your edges to bite in, so you can steer your skis and brake. When you are turning on firm snow, the edges of your skis ride over the snow. Firm snow is the most common snow condition found at a ski resort and can provide the easiest learning conditions.

TYPES OF FIRM SNOW
There are several types of firm snow:
1. **Skier-compacted snow** has been compacted by constant skier traffic.
2. **Groomed (corduroy) snow** has been groomed by a snow-grooming machine. These machines are driven up and down the mountain, levelling and texturing the snow's surface. The resulting groomed surface is known as **corduroy** as it resembles the appearance of corduroy fabric. The snow surface left by the machine is dependent on the original snow quality, the weather, and the skill of the driver. One day, corduroy may be icy and unpleasant to ski; another day it may be totally delightful, like skiing on a velvet carpet.
3. **Packed-powder** is fresh snow that has been packed down by skiers or machine, but retains a degree of softness that makes it easy to ski on.
4. **Wind-packed snow** is snow that has fallen in heavy wind, which has plastered it onto the slope.
5. **Sastrugi** are snow formations that remain on a windward slope after the loose snow on top has been scoured away by the wind. The consolidated snow left behind sits in **strata-like** formations that are irregular in shape and size, but point toward the direction of the wind that formed them. Snow can **erode** to leave sastrugi a metre high in very windy locations, though 5-20 cm is more common. Sastrugi can catch your skis and make skiing difficult.

ski

skis ride on
edge in turn

firm snow

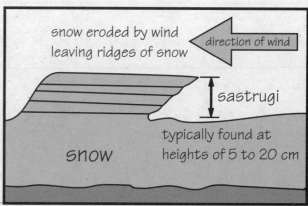

snow eroded by wind
leaving ridges of snow

direction of wind

sastrugi

snow

typically found at
heights of 5 to 20 cm

Skiing Firm Snow

PIVOTED OR CARVED TURNS

Pivoted turns are the first to learn. They are suitable for any angle of skiable slope, but are most suited to moderate to steep slopes. Use up unweighting (as the flexing and extending method) when skiing even angled slopes.

Carved turns work extremely well on firm even surfaces where the slope angle is gentle to moderate. On steeper slopes, carved turns don't give sufficient braking.

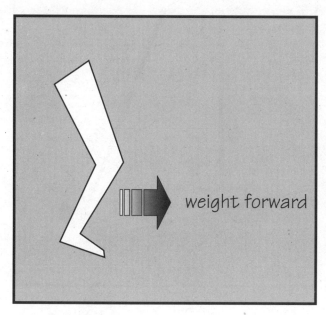

weight forward

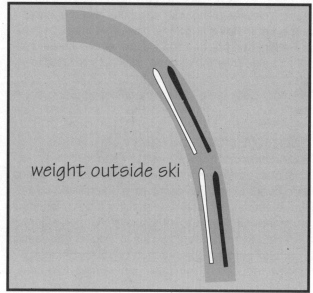

weight outside ski

WEIGHT DISTRIBUTION

Keep your weight forward to encourage more flexing in the front half of your skis. This helps the shovel to bring the ski around in the turn.

Ski with most or all of your weight distributed over the outside ski.

Skiing Ice

Ice can be found at any time of year, although it occurs mostly in the spring when the snow pack goes through melt-freeze cycles. Ice is also created by constant skier traffic, when there hasn't been a fresh snowfall for a while. Skiers compact the snow, which forms an icy surface. Ice gives little grip and minimal braking. This makes it difficult to balance and brake sufficiently.

SHARP EDGES

When you are skiing powder, sharp edges are not important as the snow is so soft. On ice, sharp edges make it possible to cut into the ice to gain some grip. Bevelling your edges to give a sharper edge angle helps further (for more information on bevelling see pages 140-2). Blunt edges cause your skis to skid over the surface, making it difficult to steer them and maintain balance. Well-tuned skis are your best line of defence against skidding on ice.

PIVOTED OR CARVED TURNS

Expert skiers can use carved turns to ski icy sections. Carved turns reduce the amount your skis skid over the ice. The problem is that carved turns are a fast method of skiing, making them unsuitable on steeper slopes and for less experienced skiers.

Pivoted turns cause your skis to skid as they bring your skis across your direction of travel. Skidding can be reduced by minimising the amount you pivot your skis.

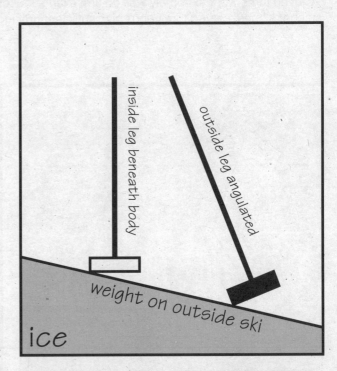

inside leg beneath body

outside leg angulated

weight on outside ski

ice

WEIGHT YOUR OUTSIDE SKI

Weighting only one ski enables that ski to cut deeper into the ice as all your body weight is concentrated on only one edge. This works more effectively than spreading your weight over two skis.

WIDEN YOUR STANCE

Angulate your outside leg as normal, but position your inside leg more directly **under** your body. If your outside leg slips away from you, your inside leg can take your weight, giving you a second chance to maintain balance.

Skiing Crust

Crust is a firm but fragile snow layer that sits above softer snow. It is a snow condition that is desperately hard to ski. I always try to ski elsewhere if possible.

INCONSISTENCY OF CRUST
Crust is usually called 'breakable crust' as it breaks under your body weight, causing you to drop through the surface layer into the soft snow beneath. It is also know as 'variable breakable crust' as the surface is so variable in strength. Sometimes you break through and other times you don't. This inconsistency makes it extremely difficult to ski and anticipation is impossible.

WEIGHT DISTRIBUTION
Weight distribution varies widely in an attempt to maintain balance. By weighting your skis equally you spread your weight over a larger surface area, so you are less likely to break through the crust. If you weight only the outside ski, it will tend to break through, knocking you off balance. When on the surface, try to keep your weight forward; when under the crust, do what you can.

PIVOTED OR CARVED TURNS
Pivoted turns enable you to keep your speed down, so you can maintain balance when you break through the crust.

WALKING ON RICE PAPER
One way to ski breakable crust is to treat it gently, as if you were walking on rice paper and trying not to tear it. By gently up unweighting and gently making the transition you may be able to keep on the surface.

SKI HEAVILY
If skiing gently still causes you to break through, try the opposite approach and ski heavily. Smash through the crust with each turn by jumping onto it. This is a desperate measure to take as it demands so much energy, but at least turning is more consistent.

Use vigorous up unweighting to get you back on the surface of the snow so you can execute the transition stage of the turn.

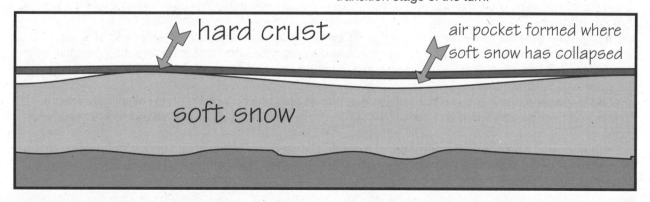

hard crust

air pocket formed where soft snow has collapsed

soft snow

Skiing Soft Snow

MORE INFO

Soft snow is a three-dimensional medium. With firm snow, you ski on its **surface**, riding on the **edges** of your skis to turn. With soft snow you ski **through** it, riding on a platform of snow under the **bases** of your skis.

DEFINITIONS

Skiers talk about snow being light or heavy in reference to the **weight** of snow, when technically they should be referring to **density**. Density is the mass of snow per unit volume. Snow with a lower density has a higher ratio of air in the snow pack. Crystal shape, and amount of compaction by the wind, affect density.

In this book I have used the standard skier terminology. Light means low density snow; heavy means high density snow.

TYPES OF SOFT SNOW

There are several types of soft snow:

1. **Powder** snow is light and dry. It occurs when the snow falls in low or nil wind, so the delicate crystals do not become broken or compacted.

Even though powder snow may be over a metre deep, you can ski through it as easily as if you are walking through feathers.

2. **Champagne powder** is ultra light powder. At its lightest it consists of about 3% water and 97% air.

3. **Porridge/elephant snot** are some of the terms used to describe snow that is heavier than powder. Heavier snow is often wetter snow, or snow that has been compacted by the wind. As the names suggest, the snow can be challenging to ski.

4. **Wind-deposited snow** is snow that builds up in the lee area of a mountain. Wind collects snow from current and/or previous storms and dumps it in sheltered areas. These areas are usually highly avalanche prone.

5. **Crud/chopped up snow** is the snow surface created when many skiers pass through deep snow. The inconsistency of the snow makes it demanding to ski. Crud is also the name given to any snow that is considered undesirable.

Skiing Soft Snow

MORE INFO

WHERE TO FIND THE LIGHTEST POWDER

For many skiers, powder skiing is the ultimate ski experience and they dream of light waist-deep snow on an untracked mountain.

On a powder day the snow can become 'tracked out' very quickly as the keen 'powder hounds' are up early in the morning and out hunting for the deepest and lightest snow.

One key thing to watch for is signs of wind. Snow that falls in a wind becomes compacted, so is heavy to ski. If you can find snow that fell in little or no wind, it will be lighter. Snow is often lighter amongst trees for this reason.

Altitude is also a key factor in the search for powder. Usually a fresh snowfall is deeper and lighter at higher altitudes, where the temperature is often colder and the humidity drier. Low down, the fresh snowfall is often wetter and heavier and more prone to consolidating quickly with daytime temperatures. But sometimes the best snow is found lower on the mountain, particularly if it has been windy.

Experience enables you to make sense of a few clues as to where the best snow might be. However, I never cease to be amazed at how unpredictable it is to find the best snow. Sometimes it is simply best to ski around and see what you find.

SNOW DEPTH & LIGHTNESS

When you ski through powder, you may be floating through boot-deep, knee-deep or even waist-deep snow. The amount you sink into the snow depends on the **depth** and **lightness** of the snow.

If the new snowfall is only five to ten centimetres deep, you won't be floating because it's too shallow. Instead your skis' edges will still be in contact with the firm snow beneath.

BOTTOMING OUT

'Bottoming out' is when your skis intermittently make contact with the firm snow below while skiing through soft snow.

TEST TO SEE IF THE SNOW IS WET OR DRY

Using both hands, scoop up some snow and squeeze it into a ball. If it clumps together, it's wet; if it remains loose, it's dry.

Snow that doesn't clump is easier to ski through.

'powder skiing is the ultimate ski experience for most skiers'

Skiing Soft Snow

MORE INFO

FLOATATION POINT

If your weight is positioned forward, your ski tips will nose-dive into the snow. If you sit back on your skis, you will skid around on the tails. Inbetween the two is a sweet spot, **the 'floatation point'**, where your skis work most effectively.

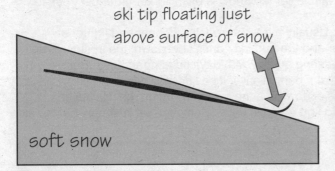

ski tip floating just above surface of snow

soft snow

CUT ONE TRENCH

Keep your legs a little closer together than usual when skiing in deep snow, to ensure that they cut only one trench. If your legs separate, your skis will more easily waver off course as it takes more strength to control them.

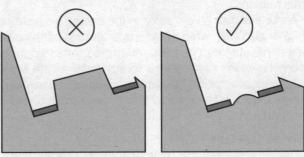

SIDEWAYS BALANCE

Weight your skis so that both sit in the snow at the same depth. If one ski supports all your weight, it will sink in the snow and throw you off balance.

Having both skis at the same depth also ensures that they are skiing through the same layer of snow, so hopefully they behave similarly.

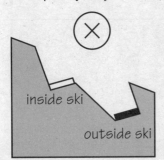

inside ski

outside ski

PITCH OF SLOPE

Skiing through deep snow will slow you down, particularly if the snow is heavy. As you ski, a pile of snow will build in front of your legs and slow you down even more. When skiing deep snow, you need a slope with a suitably steep pitch. Turning on a gentle slope may bring you to a standstill in some conditions.

snow piles up in front of legs

Skiing Soft Snow

PIVOTED OR CARVED TURNS

Pivoted turns work in any soft snow condition, whether light powder or crud. On gentle slopes the amount of pivoting will be minimal, becoming more extensive to brake on steeper slopes.

Carved turns are fun in soft snow, giving smooth fast turns. But they are not so suitable for steeper slopes or difficult soft snow, like crud or porridge.

PIVOTING

As you pivot your skis during the transition stage of the turn, your skis swing around toward the direction of the next turn. On firm snow they can swing unhindered, but in deep snow they have to displace snow as they rotate, which takes more energy. Skiing in deep snow is generally more energetic than skiing on a firm surface.

UNWEIGHTING

Up unweighting is the most useful flexing and extending technique for skiing any deep snow.

As you extend to unweight in powder you push against a soft medium, which absorbs some of your energy. To compensate, take a deeper flex than usual. This gives you a **longer** extension. This enables you to compress a **platform** of snow underneath your skis, which you can push against.

Use your poles to aid unweighting.

Use terrain unweighting when you see suitable roll overs, as this makes unweighting less tiring.

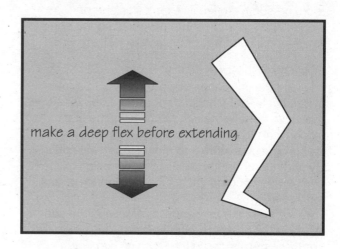

make a deep flex before extending

WHO IS IN CONTROL, YOU OR THE SNOW?

In soft snow, it can sometimes feel as if the snow has taken charge, particularly when it is heavy or cruddy and chopped up. When skiing in such conditions, ski it **powerfully**, **precisely** and with **determination**. It takes the right attitude to make your way through.

If you feel that your skis are running away from you, or the snow feels 'catchy', check that you are **completing** each turn by making deep short radius turns rather than shallow or long radius ones. Deep turns will keep your speed down to a safe manageable level. Shallow turns, in contrast, will cause you to accelerate and lose control.

Oh, and by the way, watch out for snow snakes. They grab your skis when you least expect it.

Skiing Spring Snow

In spring, the sun travels higher above the horizon than during the winter, so it's more effective in melting the snow. Spring snow that has melted by just the right amount can provide delightfully easy skiing conditions. Spring snow can make your skiing look good and is sometimes called **ego snow** for that reason.

MELT-FREEZE CYCLE

During the spring months the snow pack often goes into a **melt-freeze** cycle of melting in the daytime and re-freezing at night. During this cycle the early morning snow will be hard and icy, needing the morning sun to soften it. After a little sun on the slopes, the snow turns into delightful spring snow, which consists of wet granular sugar-like grains.

FOLLOW THE SUN

To avoid the icy slopes that are created in a melt-freeze cycle, note the sun's position. Look for slopes that have been in the sun for a while. The first slopes start to soften around mid-morning. As the day progresses more and more slopes will soften. By mid-afternoon, the slopes that were first to melt sometimes become too slushy, making them less easy to ski.

You can find the best snow by following the sun. When in the **northern hemisphere**, start skiing the **south-eastern** faces in the morning, working around toward **south-western** slopes later in the day. When in the **southern hemisphere**, start skiing the **north-eastern** faces, and work your way around toward **north-western** slopes.

SUN, AIR TEMPERATURE & WIND

Melting occurs most rapidly on clear days with warm air temperatures and no wind. Cloud, low air temperatures and wind all reduce the amount of melting that takes place.

OVERCOOKED SNOW

When the melt-freeze cycle is happening, the skiing can be excellent. If however the snow melts too much it becomes 'overcooked' and the snow turns to **slush**, giving challenging conditions. On a warm spring day, slopes that are exposed to the sun can become overcooked late in the day. Usually less cooked slopes can be found.

If the snow fails to re-freeze at night, further melting the next day can cause the snow to turn quickly to slush. At the opposite extreme, slopes can re-freeze very quickly after the sun has gone off the slope.

TECHNIQUE

The technique is very similar to skiing soft snow. The difference is that in soft snow you are constantly keeping in tune with the floatation point, whereas in spring snow your skis are often riding on the firm layer beneath, rather than floating. This means you can keep your weight forward as you ski without your tips nose-diving into the snow.

PIVOTED OR CARVED TURNS

In spring snow pivoted or carved turns are suitable. But pivoted turns are needed to brake on steeper slopes.

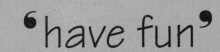

'have fun'

This chapter explains how you can vary the basic parallel technique so you can ski bumps, steeps and gunbarrels.

It also explains skiing two other types of terrain: trees and glaciers. These do not need any further techniques, but do require additional knowledge to ski safely.

Finally, the chapter explains how to jump on skis.

NOTE: This chapter assumes you have read the previous three chapters.

Bumps are skier-made mounds of snow that lie in symmetrical patterns on some skifield slopes. Bumps are also known as **moguls.** In North America they are usually called bumps. In Europe they are generally known as moguls. Both terms are used extensively and interchangeably. Skiing bumps is a sport in its own right, called **freestyle skiing**. There are two techniques of skiing bumps at a recreational level.
The two techniques are:
1. Skiing the tops.
2. Skiing the ruts.

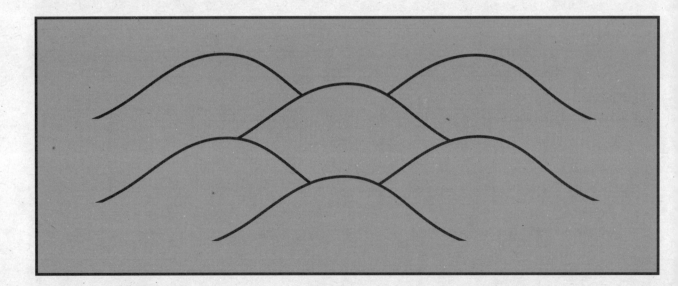

HOW BUMPS ARE MADE
Bumps are formed from the plumes of snow thrown up from the tails of skiers' skis when they turn. After a fresh snowfall, patterns quickly emerge in the snow. Soon small bumps start to form as skiers take similar lines down the slope. Once established, they quickly grow, getting bigger with the descent of every skier. Note that bumps are made by skiing the ruts between the bumps, not by skiing over them.

Skiing the Tops

If you are new to bump skiing, you can acquaint yourself with the uneven terrain by first learning to turn on the tops of small bumps. Note that it is impractical to turn on the tops of larger bumps.

PIVOTED OR CARVED TURNS
Pivoted turns are used in all bump skiing. Carved turns are for even surfaces.

TURNING ON THE TOPS OF THE BUMPS
The top of the bump can help you in two ways:
1. Can you recall driving over the crest of a hill and getting that feeling of weightlessness as you do so? Skiing over a bump works the same way; your weight automatically comes off your skis. When skiing slowly, **terrain unweighting** in this way takes the effort out of flexing and extending. When you learn to ski faster through the moguls, the bumps give you too much lift. To compensate, you can revert to using **leg retraction** to soak up the excess lift as you ski over the mogul.
2. When you are positioned on the top of the bump, the tip and tail of your skis have plenty of clearance. This enables your skis to pivot freely without catching on any snow.

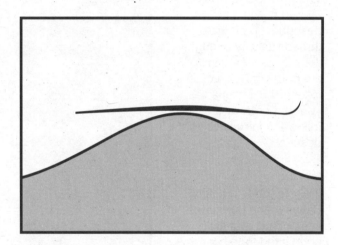

WEIGHT DISTRIBUTION
When turning in the bumps, always keep your weight forward, so you are over the top of your skis. The uneven nature of the bumps causes your weight to be thrown back onto the tails of your skis. If you learn to anticipate this, it is easier to keep your weight forward. When your weight is thrown to the rear, it puts you in the back seat, causing you to skid around on the tails of your skis, making it impossible to steer them.

COMMITMENT TO TURN
It is easy to traverse right across a bump field and not make a single turn. The next bump always looks more inviting and possibly easier than the bump you are on, until you get there. Then the next bump looks easier, and so on. To commit to a turn, plant a pole. If you can shift your focus onto your poling rather than turning, you may find it easier to keep the turns following one after the other. Whispering pole-pole-pole to yourself as you ski can help focus your attention and give you rhythm.

Skiing the Ruts

MORE INFO

Learning to ski the moguls well takes time and practice. Skiing in the ruts is an advanced parallel technique. The aim is to be able to follow the fall line through a mogul field by skiing the **ruts** in-between the bumps. When you follow the rut line you never ski over the tops of the bumps.

THE LINE

The Line is a term used by bump skiers to describe a path that threads its way through the bumps. The line is the path your **skis** must follow. The line enables your upper body to follow the fall line as you descend.

IDENTIFYING THE LINE

Between the bumps are lines of ruts that are connected together like a **zigzag staircase**. The art of finding a good line is to pick out a row of ruts that are even and uniform in size.

Watch other bump skiers to see where the lines go. Watching from above the run gives the best view of where they turn. With a little practice, the lines become easier to see.

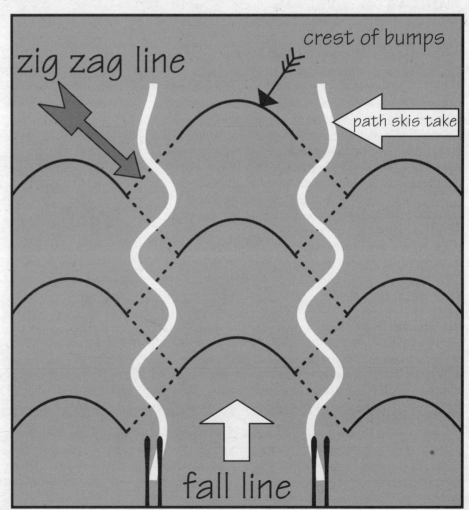

zig zag line

crest of bumps

path skis take

fall line

Skiing the Ruts

MORE INFO

SHAPE OF THE RUTS

Following the rut line takes you through undulating terrain. Small bumps have shallow troughs in the rut line that are flat rather than scooped out. Where the bumps are larger, the troughs are deeper and more scooped out, making them more demanding to ski.

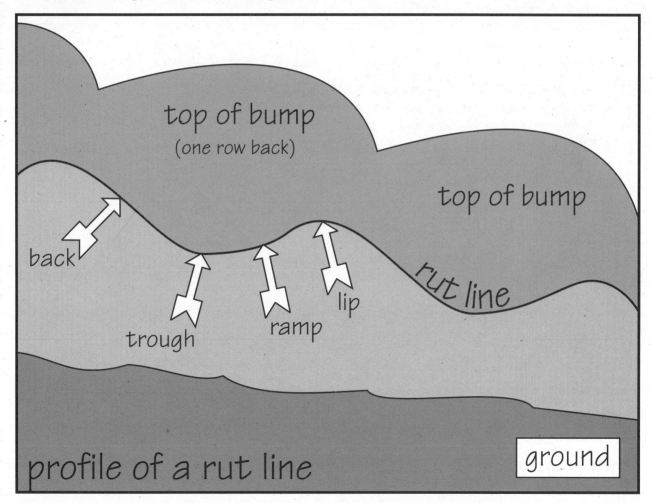

top of bump
(one row back)

top of bump

back

rut line

trough

ramp

lip

ground

profile of a rut line

Skiing the Ruts

MORE INFO

BALANCE
Skiing through uneven terrain makes it difficult to keep your weight forward. If your weight is thrown backward your skis become very difficult to control, so concentrate on keeping your weight forward. While your weight is forward on your skis, you are in the best position to steer them. Anticipating how the terrain will affect you helps you keep one step ahead.

BALANCE AT THE LIP
At the lip, the slope levels off and starts to drop away. This causes your skis to accelerate. If you let this happen unchecked your weight will be thrown onto the tails of your skis. Compensate by pulling your feet backward as they reach the lip. Remember to anticipate.

BALANCE ON THE BACK OF THE BUMP
When you descend the back of the rut, your skis will continue to accelerate. Keep your weight forward. Remember to anticipate.

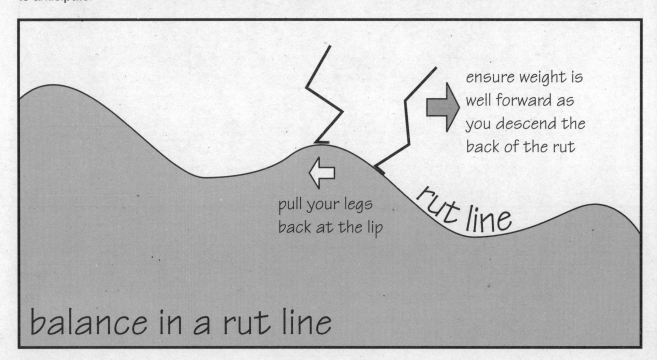

ensure weight is well forward as you descend the back of the rut

pull your legs back at the lip

rut line

balance in a rut line

Skiing the Ruts

FLEXING & EXTENDING

Use **leg retraction** as the flexing and extending technique in the bumps. This allows you to soak up the undulating terrain with your legs, preventing your upper body from being bounced around.

SEQUENCE

This sequence is based on leg retraction as the flexing and extending method.

Flexing: Flex your legs as you ascend the ramp and bring your legs under your body. Flexing stops you being thrown outward when you reach the lip.

Poling: As your feet reach the lip, **plant** your pole.

Pivoting: Immediately after the lip, your weight is released from the base of your skis as the slope drops away. This is the transition point of the turn where you **pivot** your skis.

Extending: As you ski down the back of the rut you have the opportunity to extend your legs and angulate them to make the next turn. Entering the hollow with your legs **extended** enables you to flex as you go up the next ramp.

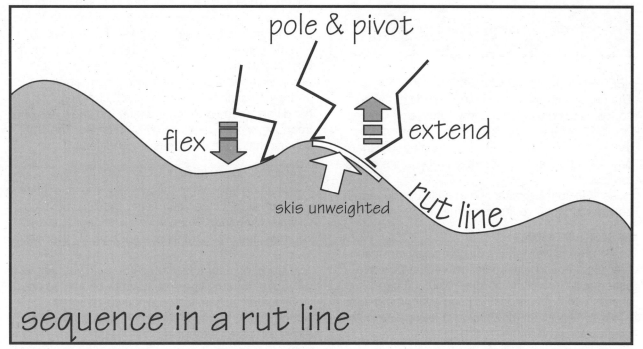

sequence in a rut line

SPEED AND BRAKING

When skiing bumps you have less opportunity to brake than when skiing an even slope. As you descend the back of the rut it is hard to brake effectively. The majority of braking has to be done in the **hollow** (trough) of the rut. To compensate, brake hard when you get the chance by driving your edges hard into the snow.

CHECK YOUR SPEED DURING EACH TURN

Once your speed increases, it is hard to slow down again. Try to ski through the bumps and control your speed with each turn.

> 'control your speed'

KEEPING YOUR SKIS ON THE SNOW

The uneven nature of the bumps tends to cause your skis to come off the snow. When up in the air you cannot steer your skis, so you may come out of the line you are following. Up in the air you cannot brake, and on landing you may find you are going too fast.

Use sufficient leg retraction to soak up the terrain so you can keep your skis on the snow.

ASSERTIVE POLING

To ski bumps well requires high energy input and precision. Poling with an **assertive** and **positive** action suits the nature of bump skiing. It can sharpen your precision and keep your timing tight.

To avoid shoulder rotation, don't leave your pole planted too long.

FACE DOWN THE FALL LINE

Always keep your upper body facing down the fall line. Remember to look where you want to go.

CROSSED SKIS

If your tips or tails become crossed, taking your weight off your skis by leg retraction (quickly flexing your legs) can help you to uncross them. If you are quick.

EASIEST CONDITIONS

Bumps are easiest to learn when the snow is soft, because it is easier to brake to a manageable speed. When it is icy, it is harder to brake, as your edges don't grip so well. In icy conditions it is all too easy to gather too much speed and lose balance.

In the spring, snow that has frozen overnight and then softened in the morning sun is excellent for bump skiing and gives the easiest conditions.

A fresh snowfall usually brings challenging conditions in the bumps, but after the snow has been packed down a little by other skiers, the soft surface that is left gives easier conditions.

LEARN TO SKI ONE RUT AT A TIME

Try teaching yourself to follow just two consecutive ruts then stop. Once you master two ruts move on to three, then four. When you can ski four in a row you may find you can, all of a sudden, ski twenty-four.

By stopping after a few turns you train yourself to pull out of a bump line. You need to be able to do this so you can safely stop when you want to, without being bounced around, at the mercy of the other bumps on either side of you.

The steeps are slopes that are over 45 degrees in gradient. Learning to ski steep slopes comes with considerable experience and expertise. The **jump turn** technique used to ski these slopes can be practised on more gentle slopes and on short steep sections where the consequences of a fall are not serious. This section will give you an insight into the way expert skiers think before skiing in steep places.

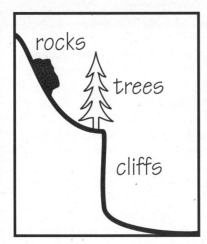

RUN OUT

Skiing on very steep slopes means that you could slide a long way before stopping. Run out is the path your falling body would take if you fell.

Here are some points that you may want to consider when assessing a run out:

1. Where would you stop if you fell? The ideal run out is a concave slope that becomes shallower. This type of slope can gradually slow you down.

2. Are there any cliffs below the slope that you could fall over?

3. Are there any obstacles on the way down, such as trees or rocks, that you could hit?

4. When skiing chutes that run between rock bands, establish if they have they a dog leg (bend) in them? If you fell above the dog leg would you slide into the rock wall to the side?

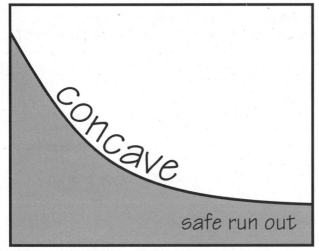

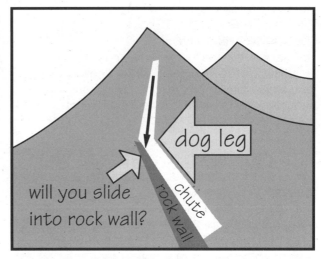

SNOW CONDITIONS

Steep slopes can only be skied under certain snow conditions. Part of the skill of skiing these slopes is learning to evaluate safe conditions.

Slopes can become totally unskiable when icy as it is impossible to get enough grip. A fall on a steep icy slope could be fatal as the fall would be fast and hard.

Soft or spring snow can be ideal if the snowpack is stable and the soft snow not too deep.

Stability of the snowpack is a prime concern when venturing on steep slopes. Will the slope avalanche? Be aware that avalanches do happen, even within the perimeter of a ski resort. Any snow slope over 25 degrees may avalanche.

Understanding avalanche conditions is something else that a skier needs to learn for their own safety. Evaluating snow stability requires a combination of training and experience.

CHECKING THE SLOPE

To evaluate a slope fully you may need to climb it first. This enables you to check the snow condition and other hazards on the route. This requires mountaineering experience and equipment.

CHECK OUT THE ABILITY OF YOUR SKI PARTY

When skiing in steep places, check that you are well aware of your own abilities and those of the rest of your party. All the party has to be able to ski the slope within a safe comfort zone. I only ski in steep areas with people I know and have skied with.

DECISION-MAKING CHECKLIST

Here are some useful questions that you may want to consider before skiing steep slopes. Hypothetical answers are given to illustrate the questions.
1. What are the **hazards**? (e.g. avalanche; ice).
2. What **events** could take place in this situation? (e.g. a fall; burial under snow).
3. What would be the **immediate consequences** of these events? (e.g. victim in state of shock; broken bones; death).
4. What would be the **rescue plan**? (e.g. find the victim; get help).
5. What would be the **long term consequences**? (e.g. loss of interest in skiing; loss of mobility of limb; death).
6. What **skills** are needed? (e.g. skiing to advanced level; avalanche awareness and survival skills).
7. What practical **precautions** can be taken? (e.g. use of avalanche beacon; carry a shovel; wearing warm clothes; ski one at a time).
8. What is the **likelihood** of these events and consequences, considering skills and precautions? (e.g. unlikely; very likely).
9. What are the **reasons** for taking the risk? (e.g. have to get from a to b; fun; satisfy the ego; afraid to decline).
10. What are the **alternatives**? (e.g. ski elsewhere; have a coffee; walk a long way to get back home).
11. How do you expect your current **emotions** to affect your performance? (e.g. help; hinder).
12. What does your **intuition** saying? (e.g. ski it; don't ski it).

Make a Choice

JUMP TURNS

Jump turns enable you to ski on steep terrain by jumping your skis around to point in the opposite direction. They are an extension of the basic pivoted turn i.e. pivoted turns with a lot of pivoting and a lot of up unweighting.

Jump turns allow you to ski in very narrow places. It is possible to turn in spaces that are only a little wider than the length of your skis.

TECHNIQUE

Start Position:
Start with your skis across the fall line.

Face outward down the slope by twisting your upper body, so your shoulders are almost parallel with your skis, this winds your body up like a spring to help you pivot your skis in the air.

Your uphill leg should be forward, to stagger your skis.

Sequence:
1. Position your weight forward, and allow your skis to slide forward a little.
2. Flex your legs and plant your pole.
3. Extend upward as if jumping and jump outward into the void. Jumping outward helps your tails clear the slope as your skis swing round.
4. In the air pivot your skis 180 degrees. Keep your pole planted for balance.
5. Land on the snow and push your knees into the slope so your edges can grip.

PAUSING AND FLOWING

When the situation is difficult, it is easier to pause between turns. When you are more in control, you can flow from one turn to the next.

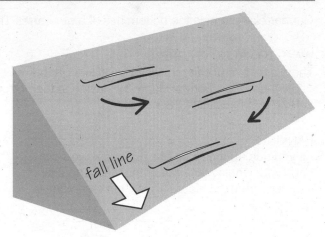

fall line

SIDE-SLIPPING

Side-slipping is used to pass over sections of terrain that are too difficult to turn on. When entering a gully, or when at the top of any steep slope, side slipping is a useful way to get a feel for the snow before committing to a turn.

SIDE-STEPPING DOWN

In a situation where you are in a gully and it becomes too icy to ski or side slip, you can revert to carefully side-stepping down it, with careful use of poles for support. Not a good situation to be in.

SAFE SPOTS

When skiing in a narrow confined gully, or other hazardous areas, ski one at a time. When stopping to let another person ski, always ensure you stop in a **safe spot**, where you will not be swept away by an avalanche or by another skier crashing into you.

Gunbarrels

Gunbarrels resemble the bottom half of a gunbarrel. They are also know as **half pipes**.

WAYS TO SKI GUNBARRELS

There are several different ways to ski in a gunbarrel.
1. Ski them like a normal slope, by staying in the bottom of the barrel.
2. Ride up the sides of the barrel.

BANKING

As you ride up the sides of a gunbarrel, you can bank your whole body, rather than just angulating your legs from the hips. This is a fun technique in gunbarrels.

JUMPING

If you ride up the sides of a gunbarrel, you can jump from the lip and either land outside the barrel or turn in the air and land back inside it. Watch other skiers to get the idea.

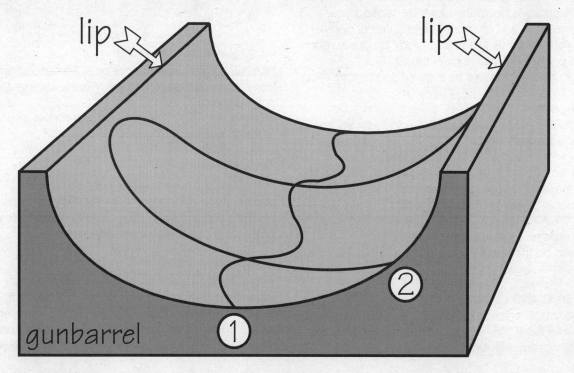

Areas of trees offer exhilarating skiing, and often the lightest snow after a powder dump. There is always less wind amongst trees, so the snow falls more gently onto the ground, giving lighter snow.

LOOK AT THE GAPS
The trick to skiing the trees is not to hit them. Here is a tip that may sound too good to be true, but it works.

If you look at the trees, they tend to loom up on you, closer and closer, then bang, too late. Alternatively if you look at the gaps between the trees, you will find it much easier to ski past them.

When in the forest, look well ahead, and choose a **gap line** that offers good skiing.

VERBAL COMMUNICATION
It can be hard to see people in the trees so verbal communication is often most effective.

If you carry a whistle when you ski in the trees, you will have a better chance of being found if you need help.

BUDDY SYSTEM
If you have an accident amongst the trees, it could take a long while before anyone realises that you are missing, and longer still to find you.

When skiing in the trees you can take an extra safety precaution by setting up a **buddy system**, where you and a friend agree to keep in contact when skiing a stretch of trees.

Useful details to agree on include:
1. Where you expect to emerge from the trees.
2. How far you will ski between contact points. e.g. You could arrange to catch up every twenty turns.
3. What happens if you cannot find each other? Are you both OK or has your buddy had an accident? Making a plan to cover this possibility can save much time and confusion later on. You could decide on a meeting place in a building where you can wait out of the weather and contact rescue services, if necessary.

'look at the gaps'

SPEED CONTROL
Skiing in a controlled comfortable manner allows you to stop when you need to. This reduces the likelihood of getting to know a tree more intimately.

Glaciers

Glaciers are areas where the snow/ice cover is permanent. The snow that falls on the glacier becomes compacted into ice that may be up to several hundred metres thick. Each winter, a new layer is added to the glacier. In the warmer months the snowpack decreases in size as it melts.

CREVASSES

Glaciers, despite consisting mainly of ice, flow like a very slow river. When they flow over convex terrain they **crack** as the ice is put under **tension**. These cracks are called crevasses and are a **typical** glacial feature.

  Some ski resorts include glacier skiing. When skiing on a glacier you need to be aware of crevasses, and ski with control so you can stop quickly to avoid skiing into what could be a fifty metre deep slot.

  Do not expect crevasses to be signposted. Awareness and a keen eye are needed.

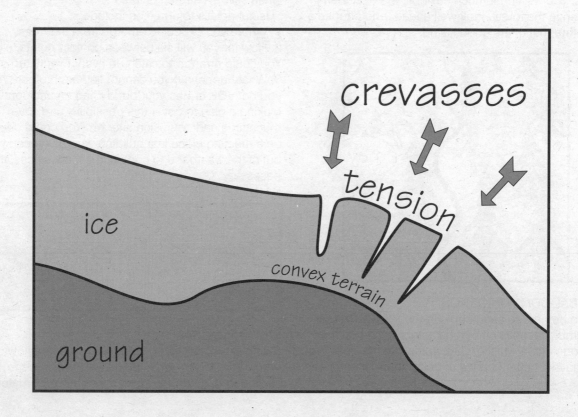

SNOW BRIDGES

When the winter snow falls and the wind blows, some crevasses that are wide open in summer become covered. The new snow falling on either side of the slot may form a bridge over the abyss. In some places these bridges can be several metres deep, even in the middle where they are weakest. In other places they may only be a few centimetres deep and not strong enough to support a person's weight.

LOOK FOR SAGGING

Skiing over a sagging area is highly dangerous as sagging is a **sure sign** that there is a crevasse underneath. Sagging occurs when the snow bridge is weak. Any additional weight may cause it to collapse. If you see lines of sagging, or small holes, expect the crevasse to **extend beyond the visible signs**.

partly formed snowbridge

SAGGING

GLACIERS AND POOR VISIBILITY

In poor visibility, when the light is flat, it may be impossible to see crevasses or signs of sagging. This is the time to ski elsewhere.

Jumping offers a lot of fun and challenges. In the air there are many different tricks that can be tried, which make the jump more challenging and exciting. This section looks at the terrain for jumping, and the approach you take on the ramp. It leaves what happens up in the air to your creativity.

There are two basic types of jump to get air from. These are:

1. Kickers
2. Rocks & cornices

SAFETY
Before jumping you need to check:
1. The suitability of the landing site.
If you cannot see the landing site, ski down and check its suitability and look for any hidden obstacles. If you decide it is OK, then side step back up the hill to jump.
2. Check that the landing site is free from other skiers.
If you cannot see the landing site, get a friend to ski down and indicate when it is clear to jump. Verbal signals can be confusing as the situation can change from one-second to the next. A raised ski pole above the head is a common indicator that the jump is clear, and quickly shows if the situation changes.

Kickers

Kickers have an approach ramp that dips before rising up to the lip of the jump. Kickers kick you up in the air as you leave the ground. They are an excellent type of jump for doing tricks in the air.

START POSITION

When choosing a start position, you need to estimate how fast you want to be going when you leave the lip. Speed depends on how high you start up the ramp and the condition of the snow.

It can be difficult to judge where to start. A useful indicator comes from the laws of physics. To make it up to the lip you must start above the height of the lip. Guess where the height of the lip is and start a little higher.

CONTROLLING THE DESCENT

As you ski down the approach ramp to the lip, use the snowplough to check your speed if you are going too fast.

THE POP

The **pop** is a technique to project you upward and outward from the lip. At the lip you do not need an excessive amount of speed, but what is more important is a good pop to get you up into the air. Technique:

1. **Flex** your legs as you approach the lip.
2. At the lip make the pop by **extending** your legs.
3. As you extend, **project** your chest forward, as if you were crossing the finish line of a race.
4. Use your arms to fine-tune balance.

Pushing your chest forward puts your weight forward. Projecting your weight forward counteracts the nature of a kicker jump to throw you back.

TO REDUCE THE HEIGHT OF YOUR JUMP

If you feel you have too much speed as you approach the lip, you can reduce the height of your jump by **flexing** instead of extending at the lip.

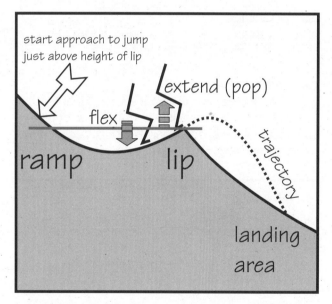

start approach to jump just above height of lip

extend (pop)

flex

ramp   lip

trajectory

landing area

THE LANDING

Land with your knees slightly bent.

Choose a jump that has a downhill landing. A downhill sloping landing enables you to land with less impact as it slopes in the direction you are falling. If you have a steep landing site you can take bigger jumps with greater safety.

Flat landings are hard on the body, and are best avoided.

Rocks & Cornices

MORE INFO

Jumping from rocks and cornices is different from jumping from kickers. The take off is much slower and tricks are not usually done in the air.

CHECK THE PROFILE OF THE ROCK
Ensure that it is practical to clear the rock. If it slopes outward below you, you may land on rock rather than snow. Not a good idea.

AS YOU JUMP
Just as you are about to leave contact with the snow, flex your legs to lower your body.

THE TAKE OFF
An ideal jump site is one that is almost flat at the top, with just a gentle incline to give you enough speed to leave the top cleanly without scraping any rocks on the way.

LANDING
Land with your knees slightly bent.

The landing site should be suitably steep to make it safe to jump. **A flat landing is dangerous** as the impact on your body could cause you injury.

Powder days are best for jumping from rocks or cornices as the landings are softer and a lot more forgiving.

STABILITY OF CORNICE
When jumping from a cornice, you need to evaluate how stable the cornice is before you jump from it. I had the experience of a cornice breaking off behind my skis. The cornice dropped four metres onto the slope beneath, which then avalanched. Not a good situation to be in.

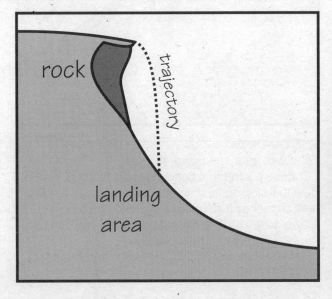

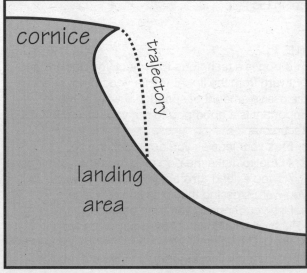

Skis
  Checking Skis
  Types of Skis
  Ski Length
  Ski Width
  Ski Flex
Boots
  Boot Options
  Forward Lean
  Forward Flex
  Ramp Angle
  Fitting Boots
Bindings
  Setting Bindings
  Binding Notes
  Lifter Plates
Poles
Functional Clothing
  Multi-Layer System
  Extremities
  Sunglasses & Goggles

This chapter will help you understand your ski equipment. It explains the pros and cons of different equipment options, and the benefits of different features. It gives you practical information to help you when you next buy some gear.

Skis look fairly similar, but can feel totally different in use. One pair may feel great while another pair may feel awful. Skis that suit a beginner are totally different from those that suit an expert. Skis suitable for certain snow conditions or types of terrain also differ. The ski market is such that there is plenty of choice, so you can expect to find something that suits you.

NEW OR SECOND-HAND

New skis are always nice to have as they run smoothly, feel responsive, and may offer advantages due to new designs.

Innovations in ski design cumulate over time. From one year to the next the changes are usually imperceptible, but if you look back over five years it is easier to see the improvements that have been made.

New skis are available from ski shops, some department stores, and also some general sports shops.

Second-hand skis can give excellent skiing. Second-hand prices vary enormously, from quite expensive to free, depending on where you look. Ski shops may have second-hand skis, old rental skis or demonstration skis on sale. Specialist second-hand sports shops may stock skis. The 'For sale' column of your local newspaper, or the local advertiser, is another source. If you live near a ski area, your town may have a second-hand ski sale. These are usually held before the ski season starts. Notice boards are other sources in ski towns; look for a central notice board or one in a supermarket. If you are skiing on a budget, ask around in the town as there are always old skis needing a good home.

WHAT SKI SHOP STAFF NEED TO KNOW

For ski shop staff to help you choose suitable skis, they need to know:
1. Your weight.
2. Your height.
3. Your level of experience, such as your total number of ski days.
4. How you regard yourself as a skier: determined, relaxed, ambitious.
5. What you want to ski: bumps, groomed runs, steeps, powder, or a bit of everything.
6. How many days you expect to ski in the next three years.

ROCK SKIS

Skiing over rocks is inevitable. The worst time of year for hitting rocks is at the start of the season before there is a good snow cover, and toward the end of the season as the snow begins to melt. Rocks are most difficult to detect after a fresh snowfall, when they are hidden below a shallow layer of soft snow.

I like to have an old pair of skis to use as 'rock skis' when too many rocks are showing. This avoids base damage to newer skis.

Checking Skis

MORE INFO

Second-hand skis can have all sorts of defects that you may miss in a casual glance. New skis can also have faults. Checking before buying is much easier than negotiating afterward. Here are some questions to help you check for damage (some do not apply to new skis).

BASES
1. What is their general state?
2. How much have they been used?
3. Are they damaged? If base damage has been repaired properly, there is not usually a problem. If water has entered the ski through an un-repaired hole, the expansion and contraction of water as it freezes and thaws can damage the ski.
4. Are the bases delaminating from the skis?
5. Are there any blisters (air pockets under the base)? These are created by overheating when hot waxing.
6. Are the bases flat? If not they will need tuning.

SIDEWALLS
1. Is there any damage to the sidewalls?
2. Are there any repairs to the sidewalls?

TOP-SHEET
1. Are there any signs of damage?
2. Are there any signs of delamination of the top sheet from the rest of the ski?
3. How many old binding holes are there in the top of the ski? Too many holes, and holes drilled close together, weaken the ski.

   Mounting a binding when there is already a set of holes in the top sheet can be tricky. The binding may have to be mounted forward or back of the ideal position to ensure that holes do not coincide, or come too close together. Do you want to make this sort of compromise?

EDGES
1. How much edge is left on the ski? There should be enough to allow further base grinds and side edge sharpening.
2. Is there any damage to the edges?
3. Have any edge repairs been made?

CAMBER
1. Does the camber seem flattened, or is it similar to a new ski? Check by placing both bases together to see how much camber there is.
2. Is the camber firm? Check by squeezing bases together.

FLEX
To see how to flex skis, read page 30.
1. Is the flex of each ski the same?
2. Does the flex feel too soft or too stiff for you?

TWISTS & BENDS
Put both bases together and pinch the skis in the centre to compress the camber. If they are O.K you will not be able to see any light between the skis. Do the bases meet right up to the tips of the skis? Look carefully for any light showing just below the tips, because this is where skis often become bent.

TORSIONAL STIFFNESS
To find out how to test for torsional stiffness read page 31. Is the ski torsionally stiff or is it like a noodle?

Types of Skis

There are several different types of skis (giant slalom, slalom, all-terrain, bump, powder and super sidecut) that suit different tasks, snow and terrain. The first four appear similar in shape, while powder and super sidecut skis are noticeably different. Skis are also designed to suit different ability levels (beginners, intermediates, advanced and expert skiers). When choosing skis, decide what type of skis you want and find those designed for your ability.

CHOOSING SKIS
Choice of ski depends on:
1. What you like skiing most (powder, races, bumps, groomed cruisy runs, steeps, ice!).
2. The conditions you most often come across.
3. The conditions you find difficult (a particular ski could help you ski them better).

GIANT SLALOM (G.S) SKIS
Giant slalom skis are best suited to long radius turns and powder skiing. They have a more even flex pattern than slalom skis. Once they had less sidecut than slalom skis; today they have more.

ALL-TERRAIN SKIS
All-terrain skis are for skiers who want all-round skis that perform well in most situations, rather than specialist skis.

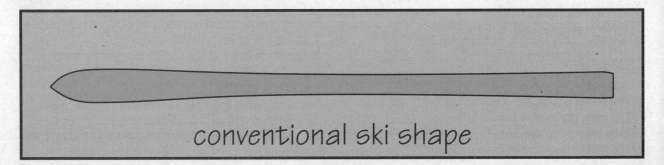

conventional ski shape

SLALOM SKIS
Slalom skis are best suited to short radius turns and bump skiing. Slalom skis have a soft shovel to help initiate the turn and a stiff tail to kick you out of one turn and into the next.

BUMP SKIS
Many bump skiers prefer slalom skis. Specialist bump skis are soft at the tip to help absorb the uneven terrain. Due to their high degree of speciality they are more suited to the bump competitor than the recreational mogul skier.

Types of Skis

MORE INFO

POWDER (FAT) SKIS

Most medium to soft even-flexing skis make good powder skis. But use of specialist powder skis (fat skis) makes powder skiing easier. These skis excel in soft snow. The extra width gives the skis good flotation (ski tips don't sink so easily) in powder. The extra width also gives a more stable platform; narrow skis are harder to balance laterally in deep snow. The disadvantage is that the extra width makes it more strenuous to edge the skis on firm snow, as you have less leverage. This makes them impractical for general use. Their soft flex, which makes them easy to turn in powder, is less effective on ice. Powder skis are often used by heli-ski companies to give easier and therefore more enjoyable powder skiing for their customers.

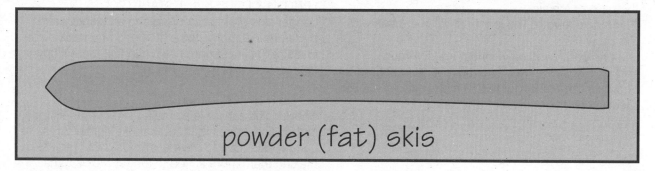

powder (fat) skis

SUPER SIDECUT (PARABOLIC, HOURGLASS) SKIS

Super sidecut skis have greater (smaller radius) sidecut than conventional skis, due to their extra width at tip and tail, narrow waist and shorter length. Their greater sidecut enables them to carve tighter turns than conventional skis, making carved turns more practical in more situations. They are less stable than conventional shaped skis when skiing in a straight line, but this is not a major disadvantage.

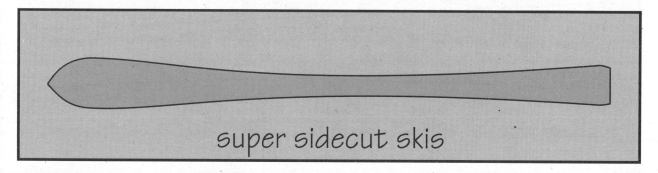

super sidecut skis

Ski Length

There are many factors involved in determining your choice of ski length.

MEASURING LENGTH

Ski length can be measured by several methods, each giving a different figure.

1. Chord length: The distance in a straight line from tip to tail.
2. Base length: The distance from tip to tail along the base of the ski.
3. Running length: The length of ski in contact with the snow.

Chord length and base length are common methods of sizing skis. Two metre skis measured by chord length are longer than 2 metre skis measured by base length.

LENGTH & BASE AREA

Increasing the length and/or width of skis increases the base area.

Skis with a larger base area travel faster and give greater flotation in soft snow.

LENGTH & FORE & AFT STABILITY

Longer skis give greater fore and aft stability and therefore feel more stable at speed and track better in a straight line. Longer skis can feel more clumsy than shorter skis when turning.

LENGTH & TURNABILITY

Shorter skis can have a smaller sidecut radius than longer skis, enabling them to make tighter turns. Longer skis have to have a larger sidecut radius, making them more suited to longer radius turns.

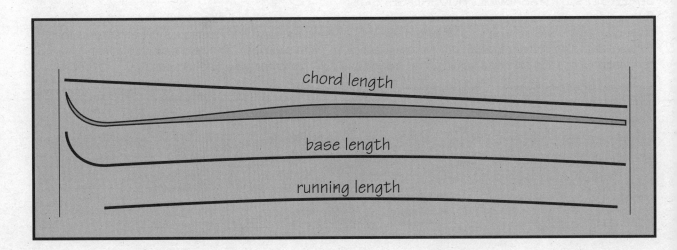

chord length

base length

running length

Ski Length

MORE INFO

LENGTH & EXPERIENCE

It is advantageous for a beginner to learn on short skis for a fast rate of progress. Short skis feel more manageable and less cumbersome than long skis to a beginner. Long skis may be good for the ego, but impair learning. It's your choice.

Advanced skiers ski faster than beginners and therefore need longer skis, which offer more stability at higher speeds, and give more fore and aft balance. The experience of advanced skiers enables them to cope with the extra length.

If you are a beginner, start short and increase ski length as you progress.

LENGTH & THE TYPE OF SKI

The ideal length of ski varies with the type of skis you choose. Some skis need to be skied longer than others. **All-terrain** and **slalom skis** are considered to be the standard length against which others are judged.

Giant slalom skis: Giant slalom turns are skied faster than slalom turns. Therefore it is advantageous to have longer skis. Longer skis go faster as they have a greater base area, are more stable at speed and track better in a straight line.

Bump skis: Bump skis are skied shorter because bump skiers need to make short sharp quick turns. Shorter skis are more manoeuvrable and have less swing weight, which facilitates quicker turns.

Parabolic & fat skis: Due to their extra width they can be shorter and still maintain the same base area. This also helps their manoeuvrability. If you want to have fun and make short turns, ski them really short.

LENGTH & BODY WEIGHT

Heavier skiers need longer skis to support their weight. Longer skis give the necessary additional base area to spread the skier's weight over a larger area of snow. This enables skiing in soft snow with adequate flotation.

LENGTH & HEIGHT

If we took two skiers of the same weight, but one twice the height of the other, the taller of the two would need a longer ski. This is because the taller skier has a higher centre of mass, which reduces stability. Longer skis give them the extra fore and aft stability they need.

LENGTH & STYLE

Skiers wanting to make shorter turns need short manoeuvrable skis. Skiers wanting to ski fast and with long radius turns need longer skis.

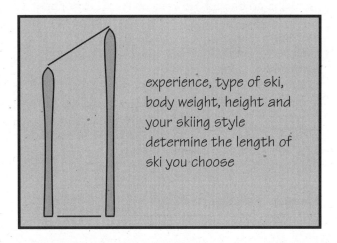

experience, type of ski, body weight, height and your skiing style determine the length of ski you choose

Ski Width

MORE INFO

Once, skis were manufactured in similar widths. Today, the width of skis varies considerably from conventional widths to that of powder (fat) skis or super sidecut skis.

WIDTH & BASE AREA
Extra width gives skis a greater base area, which makes them faster over the snow. Because of this it is recommended that wider skis be skied shorter.

Note that wider skis generally have less swing than narrower skis of the same base area, because they are shorter.

WIDTH & SIDECUT
The extra width of super sidecut skis combined with the narrow waist gives a ski with a smaller radius sidecut, enabling it to carve tighter turns. Fat skis, in contrast, have a more conventional larger radius sidecut.

WIDTH & LATERAL STABILITY
Wide skis that maintain their width under the boot (fat skis) have high lateral stability. This is advantageous when skiing powder because the skis are easier to control. However, on firm snow and ice (when the ski has to ride on its edge, rather than on a platform of snow under the base) it is difficult and tiring to edge the ski. This makes fat skis impractical for such conditions.

Super sidecut skis don't suffer from this problem because they are narrow under the boot, but don't give quite as good stability in powder.

Using lifter plates makes edging easier (read page 123 for information on lifter plates).

WIDTH & FLOTATION
Wider skis float beautifully in deep snow. This and the additional lateral stability of wide skis make them ideal for powder skiing.

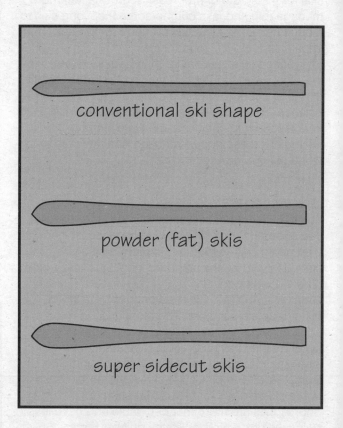

conventional ski shape

powder (fat) skis

super sidecut skis

WIDTH & EDGE-TO-EDGE TIME
A narrow ski is quicker edge-to-edge i.e. you can quickly roll the ski from one edge to the other.

Changing edges on wider skis takes longer, making it slower from turn to turn.

Ski Flex

There are several factors that determine the flex you need.

FLEX & BODY WEIGHT
A heavier skier needs stiffer skis than a lighter skier otherwise the skis will over-flex when turning. This is particularly so when skiing in soft snow because the flex of the ski is not limited by a firm surface underneath.

Skis that are too stiff will only bend a little and be hard to turn. Skis that are too soft will turn too sharply (over turn).

FLEX & SNOW CONDITION
Skis that are best suited for skiing on ice should have a stiff flex to give better grip at the tip and tail. Skis that are best suited for skiing in powder should have a soft flex that will bend more easily in a soft medium. It is impossible for one model of ski to be ideally suited to both uses. A soft ski on ice can be as difficult to ski as a stiff ski in powder.

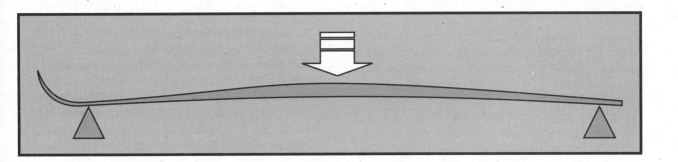

FLEX & EXPERIENCE
Beginners need soft skis that will flex at low speeds so the ski will turn. Advanced skiers need skis that will not vibrate at higher speeds. Soft skis are too prone to vibration for use by advanced skiers. Advanced skiers can flex a stiffer ski as they create greater centripetal force in the turn by skiing faster.

FLEX & STYLE
An assertive energetic skier may prefer stiffer skis as they ski hard and fast creating high centripetal forces. A more relaxed skier may prefer a softer ski that flexes more readily.

Ski boots consist of three principle parts: a rigid plastic outer shell, a plastic cuff and a soft inner boot. Ski boots should keep your feet warm, be comfortable, brace the ankle and be designed so they can be attached to the ski.

KEEPING YOUR FEET WARM

Ski boots keep your feet warm with an insulated inner boot.

Temperatures can vary considerably when skiing. Sometimes it can be warm; at other times it can plummet to minus 30 degrees Celsius or lower.

COMFORT

Ski boots have to be comfortable; any pain from your boots will immediately impair your skiing performance. Ski shop staff can fix most problems, or you can learn about tweaking boots yourself.

ANKLE SUPPORT

To give you more control over edging your skis, boots are designed with a rigid plastic shell and a high cuff to brace the ankle joint. The cuff allows you to tilt the ski precisely without relying on the strength of your ankle. The cuff only allows forward leg movement (forward flex). Movement left and right and back is virtually eliminated. Higher cuffed boots brace the leg more effectively, giving better control. A higher cuff boot generally offers more comfort to the shin as it distributes the pressure over a larger area.

BOOT BINDING INTERFACE

A universal ISO standard allows alpine ski boots to be attached to alpine skis by any ski bindings complying to the same standard (not all bindings mounted to skis will fit the full range of boot sole lengths), with only minor fitting adjustments of the binding's settings.

FOOTBEDS

Effective footbeds in ski boots are contoured to the shape of a foot sole and support the arches of your feet. By taking up space under the arches of your feet, they reduce excess foot movement within the boot. This gives a more comfortable fit and boots that feel more responsive.

Customised footbeds are available that are moulded to your feet; these may give a more comfortable fit than using standard non-custom footbeds. However, it may be optimistic to assume that they will give custom alignment of your foot to your leg. If they do give alignment, remember that your feet are inside ski boots made of rigid plastic that may override any alignment when tightened around the leg.

Note that base plates are fitted in the bottom of ski boot shells. Some designs of base plate are **flat**. These designs require that you use a footbed for arch support and comfort. Other base plate designs are **contoured** like a foot sole and give arch support and comfort in conjunction with footbeds. Note that a shaped base plate may conflict with a footbed, especially a custom-made footbed.

Remember to take out any existing footbeds before putting new ones into your inner boots.

Boot Options

MORE INFO

There are many options to consider when buying a pair of boots.

NEW OR SECOND-HAND BOOTS?

I have often bought second-hand skis, but I prefer to buy new boots. I have several concerns about buying second-hand boots:

1. Inner boots mould to the person's feet. It is therefore more difficult to find a pre-used boot that fits a second owner comfortably.
2. When buying new boots, you can choose from a wide range. When buying second-hand the choice is more limited, lessening the probability of finding a well-fitting boot.
3. Foot hygiene is also something to think about. Do you really want to inherit somebody else's smelly boots, together with their foot problems?

INNER BOOTS

Inner boots vary. Those designed for beginners tend to be softer and designed for comfort. Inner boots designed for more advanced skiers should be firmer to give better performance. Firm boots can still be comfortable, but may need a little more care in fitting.

   Custom-fitted inners are fitted to your feet by injecting foam into the inner boot, or by heating up the inner, so the padding flows around the shape of your feet. It is bit of a gamble because you only find out how comfortable they are after the process is complete, and by that time you are committed to buying them. Some inners can only be moulded once; others can be remoulded four or five times which is a definite advantage. While you are still committed to buying the boot, you at least have the opportunity to have it refitted, and have a better option of resale.

BASIC BOOT DESIGNS

There are three basic designs of ski boot:
Front-entry: Front-entry designs are similar to a conventional shoe, enabling you to open up the front of the boot to slip your foot in. The front of the boot then clips up to hold your foot secure. This design is common in boots at the top of the range.
Mid-entry: Mid-entry designs clip up like a front entry design boot, but the rear part of the cuff drops further back when unbuckled, making it easier to get your foot in and out.
Rear-entry: Rear entry designs open and close at the back of the boot.

ERGONOMICS

Boots have to be easy to use:
1. Buckles: Check if the buckles can be clipped up and adjusted with ski gloves on. Check that they have micro-adjustment so they can be finely set to the correct tension on your foot.
2. Drying boots: Check if the inner boots can be easily taken out and put back in the shells, so you can dry them out. If you have difficulty it may be because it requires a knack; ask the boot technician to try. If they struggle as well, the design is not practical.
3. Walk mode: Some boots have a walk mode for easier walking by allowing the cuff to pivot more freely at the heel when required.

Forward lean refers to the ski boot cuff angle.

THE PURPOSE OF FORWARD LEAN

To ski, you must be able to bend your legs so you can use knee angulation and flexing and extending techniques to make the transitions between turns, while being able to keep your weight forward.

Forward lean enables you to ski with your knees bent while keeping your weight forward.

If your boots didn't have forward lean, your weight would be on the tails of your skis when your legs flexed. To bring your weight forward, you would have to bend excessively from the waist, giving an impractical skiing position.

ADJUSTABLE FORWARD LEAN

Boots with adjustable forward lean are preferable because you can experiment with the settings to find an angle that you prefer.

Boots with no adjustment are OK provided they have enough lean.

Beginners' boots are often too upright. It's beginners who seem to have the most trouble initiating turns and keeping their weight forward, having to hunch over their skis to do so.

Avoid boots with a cuff that is too upright, unless being used with a tilted lifter plate (see page 123).

SETTING FORWARD LEAN

Advanced/expert skiers usually prefer greater forward lean to bring their knees forward. This gives greater leverage to steer the skis when using knee angulation. Experiment to find your preferred setting.

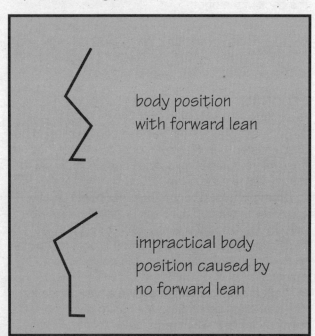

body position
with forward lean

impractical body
position caused by
no forward lean

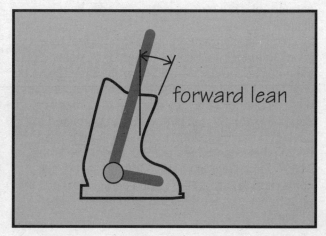

forward lean

Forward Flex

Ski boots have a cuff that pivots. When you press your shins forward into the tongues of the boots, the cuffs will pivot (flex) forward. Forward flex must have a limited range of movement because your leg can only move so far forward without injury. Boots with progressively stiffer flex are more comfortable than boots that abruptly stop flexing.

THE PURPOSE OF FORWARD FLEX

Forward flex gives **suspension** to boots. The flexing of the boot takes some of the shock out of the terrain, like shock absorbers on a mountain bike. This enables you to retain better control of your skis and makes skiing less tiring and more comfortable on your shin bones. Flex is particularly helpful when skiing bumps or landing jumps that transmit a lot of impact to your body.

When your boots flex forward in the turn you gain all the benefits of having greater forward lean.

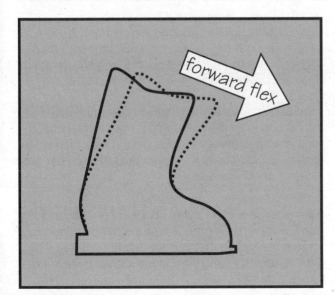

forward flex

THE RIGHT AMOUNT OF FLEX

Boot flex has to be matched to your **speed**, **weight** and **height**. All these variables affect the force that you apply to the front of the boot. A tall, heavy racer travelling fast can easily flex a stiff boot, whereas a shorter, lighter skier who is travelling more slowly would only flex a stiff boot by a fraction of its possible range of movement, so wouldn't gain the benefits of good shock absorption. Instead they would have a hard ride, like riding a mountain bike with no suspension and hard tyres. A softer option, allowing more flex, would be more appropriate. When choosing boots in a warm ski shop, remember that boot flex stiffens in cold temperatures.

ADJUSTABLE FLEX

Boots with the option to adjust flex are preferable, so you can tailor the flex to suit your body weight and typical speed range.

THIN LEGGED SKIERS

Skiers with thinner legs may find that when they tighten their boots, the overlap of the cuff is so extensive that it adds to the stiffness of the boot. People with thinner legs are often lighter and therefore need the exact opposite, i.e. a softer flexing boot. Adding padding to the rear of the inner boot can help minimise this problem by filling out the boot and causing less overlap of the cuff. This also gives additonal forward lean on front and mid-entry ski boots.

Ramp Angle

MORE INFO

Ramp angle controls ankle flex by tilting the inside floor of your ski boot shells.

THE PURPOSE OF RAMP ANGLE

Ankle joints have a limited range of forward movement. Forward lean combined with the furthermost flexing of the boot must not exceed the range of movement of the ankle joint, otherwise injury will occur. Ramp angle lifts the base of the foot at the heel, reducing the amount that the ankle joint is flexed. This effectively means that boots can have greater forward lean and flex without straining the ankle.

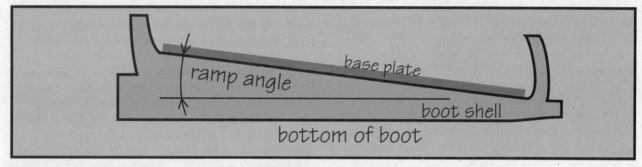

ramp angle

base plate

boot shell

bottom of boot

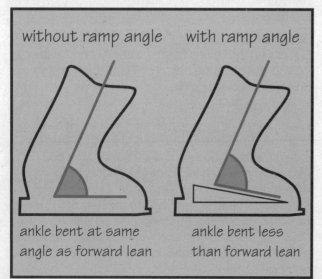

without ramp angle | with ramp angle

ankle bent at same angle as forward lean

ankle bent less than forward lean

ADJUSTABLE RAMP ANGLE

Some boots have adjustable ramp angle. If not, add padding under the heel to increase the ramp angle. Some footbeds increase the ramp angle because they are thicker in the heel than at the ball of the foot.

Adjusting ramp angle internally does not influence forward lean as the cuff angle remains the same; it only changes ankle flex. Using tilted lifter plates (see page 123) externally increases the forward lean but doesn't affect ankle flex.

SETTING ANGLE

Ramp angle is often set to take out heel lift (heel movement in the boot). Too much ramp angle may create the feeling that you are skiing on tiptoe. Too little ramp angle and your ankle joint may have to flex too much.

Fitting Boots

Each model of boot is slightly different in length and internal shape as it is made on a different mould. To find a boot that feels right for your foot, try a wide variety of different makes and models in various sizes. This may mean a lot of experimenting, but comfortable boots are priceless. Boots should be tried with the footbeds that you intend to use with them. Read pages 148-9 for information on modifying boots to fit.

CHECKING BOOT LENGTH: METHOD 1

Remove the inner boots. Wearing a **single** pair of ski socks, put your feet in the **shells** of the boots without the inner boots and stand up.

Try to insert two fingers (one on top of the other) between your heel and the back of the boot, without curling up your toes. If two fingers fit snugly, it is the correct fit. If you can only fit one finger, the boot is too short, unless you are a serious competitor looking for a very tight racing fit for performance.

A torch is useful to see what you are doing. Remember to check both feet.

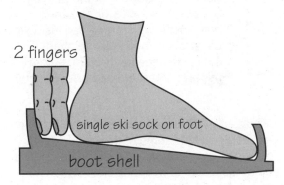

2 fingers

single ski sock on foot

boot shell

CHECKING BOOT LENGTH: METHOD 2

Wearing a **single** pair of ski socks, put your feet in just the **inner boots** and stand up. Ensure your heels are to the back. If your big toes are pressing against the end of the boots, they're too small. If your toes are not near the end, they're too big.

OTHER SIZE CHECKS

Inner boots are manufactured from soft materials that give both comfort and insulation. Due to their soft flexible nature, they **pack down** with use. A boot that is too big may often feel just right in the shop, as all the new soft padding grips your foot securely, but after a little use the boot may feel sloppy. Sloppy fitting boots give a marked lack in performance.

A boot that is too small is easier to detect, as you will feel pressure on your foot. When I have fitted a boot for length and think it is the right size. I double-check by trying boots one size smaller to see what they feel like. If these are too small I know the larger size is probably correct. Another check is to clip up the boots tightly, then check that there is plenty of provision to tighten them further (you will need to do this once the inner boot packs down). If not, the boots are too big for you.

TESTING FOR SHIN BITE & HEEL LIFT

Shin bite is the name given to sore shins. This is caused by badly fitting boots or boots that are too stiff. To test in the shop, step into a pair of skis and press you weight forward (ensure the binding springs have been set to a suitable number or you might pop straight out). The boot should feel comfortable through the whole range of movements.

The same test will detect if your heels lift in the boots. If they do, ask the ski shop staff to remedy it.

Ski bindings do two contrasting things. They must hold your feet securely on your skis, but be able to release your feet when necessary to prevent injury. Skis, being long, can act like a lever and may exert strong forces on your legs. Ski bindings are designed to release your boot from your skis before these forces become too great and cause injury.

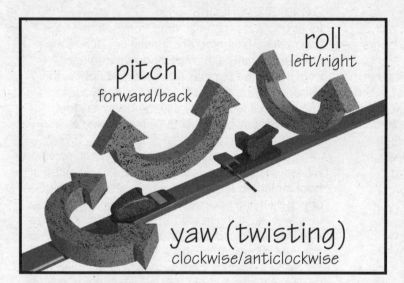

pitch
forward/back

roll
left/right

yaw (twisting)
clockwise/anticlockwise

MAINTENANCE & SAFETY CHECKS

Bindings should be regularly cleaned, lubricated (using a lubricant recommended by the manufacturer) and thoroughly checked over.
Check:
1. They release and function properly.
2. Ski brakes function.
3. They are mounted securely on the ski.
4. Fitting adjustments are correct to hold boots properly in the binding.
5. Release settings on toe and heelpieces are correct (see inside front cover of book for release chart).
6. For damage i.e. broken, deformed, missing, corroded or worn-out parts.

DIRECTIONS OF RELEASE

There are three axes of movement in which release is possible. Ideally, bindings would have the ability to release in all directions, but at present full release capability is limited to only some of these.

Yaw (twisting): All bindings enable the boot to twist out clockwise or anticlockwise. Twisting falls release from the toepiece of the binding. Some bindings have a rotating heelpiece as well to assist rotational releases. Slow twisting falls account for many injuries. The slow nature of the fall causes injury to occur before the binding can release. More dynamic, faster falls tend to flick the boots straight out of the bindings. Many slow twisting falls occur when skiing in powder and fresh snow. Ensure that your bindings are not set too high for these conditions.

Pitch: All bindings allow the boot to release forward, and some bindings have limited release backward.

Roll: Currently some bindings give limited release in the left and right roll axes. Full release would be better to help reduce injuries.

Setting Bindings

Ski boots and bindings are designed to an international standard for compatibility, but several fitting adjustments must still be made to ensure a safe interface between each boot and binding. To set your bindings to suit your boots, consult the instructions for your binding, or ask ski shop staff to help.

  The toe and heelpiece of each binding should also be adjusted to release at a certain level. An international standard exists to ensure one universal number system is used for release settings. Guidelines (ISO 11088) exist to suggest settings based on weight, height, skier type, age and boot sole length (see inside cover of book for release chart). Besides these guidelines you may want to consider any previous injuries or medical conditions. Bindings should be supplied with a chart to determine release settings.

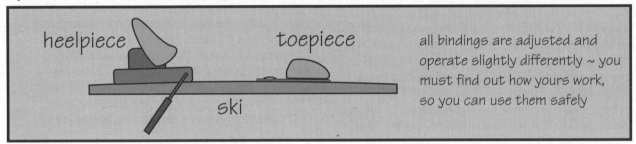

heelpiece   toepiece

ski

all bindings are adjusted and operate slightly differently ~ you must find out how yours work, so you can use them safely

TOEPIECE
Most toepieces have one position that they always return to after a fall.

HEELPIECE
Heelpieces are the part of the binding used to take your bindings on and off. The heelpiece can be:
Open (primed): ready to take a boot.
Closed: locked down to hold the boot.
  Most bindings allow you to step straight into them, though some have to be closed manually. Taking your boots out of the bindings leaves them in the open position, ready to clip straight back in next time.
  If you fall and your skis release from the toepiece, the heelpiece may still be in the closed position. You will then need to **manually open** the binding before you put your boot in.

PRE-RELEASE
A pre-release is when your binding releases unexpectedly, usually causing you to fall. The consequences of a pre-release can be as serious as those of a non-release.
  If a pattern develops of frequent pre-releases, you need to judge whether the binding needs tightening. Monitor the releases carefully. You may release only from the toepiece, or only from the heelpiece; in which case you don't need to tighten both. Only tighten half a unit at a time e.g. 6 to 6 1/2. Before increasing the setting, ensure the binding is working correctly.
  If you don't have enough knowledge to adjust your bindings safely, ask ski shop staff to do it for you.

Binding Notes

MORE INFO

NEW OR SECOND HAND

I have used many second-hand bindings with little trouble, and have seldom had anything go wrong with them. But there is always the risk that second-hand safety equipment won't work properly.

BINDING POSITION

There are different theories about positioning ski bindings. One rule of thumb is to mount the toe of the boot on the half chord. Another is to place the midpoint of the boot at a set point on the ski. These ideas conflict with each other. The first results in the toe of the boot always being in the **same** place irrespective of boot size, while the second results in the boot's toe position **varying** with boot size.

There are many variables that affect the position of bindings e.g. foot size, body weight, height, body shape, forward lean, boot flex, ski design, type of snow and terrain being skied.

With so many variables, one fixed position is a compromise. One solution is to buy a **moveable** binding that can be slid forward or backward with ease once mounted. A moveable binding enables the skier to experiment and choose the best position for them.

Moveable bindings are available as standard from some manufacturers. Other companies only sell a moveable binding to ski shops for rental skis (these bindings are moveable because they must fit the full range of boot sizes). Note that the disadvantage of many moveable bindings is their extra weight.

ANTI-FRICTION PLATE

The toe of the boot sits on an anti-friction plate. This is designed to assist release in twisting falls when there is downward pressure on the toe of the boot.

SKI BRAKES

Ski brakes drop down beneath the base of the ski when the boot is removed from the binding. Brakes prevent your skis sliding down the slope when they release. A runaway ski can be very hazardous to other skiers and inconvenient to the skier.

BLOCKING & FLEXING

Putting a boot into a binding increases the rigidity of the ski under the binding, **blocking** the amount of flex. This has an advantage and a disadvantage. The disadvantage is that the ski does not bend with a uniform arc. The flat spot created under the middle of the ski interferes with carving smooth turns. The advantage is that the blocking gives rigidity to the system and can help to reduce vibration in the ski.

Older ski bindings blocked the centre of the ski. Some later designs overcame this so the ski could **flex** more freely. Some bindings can block the ski and at the flick of a switch can allow some flexing. Blocking mode is useful for skiing in hard icy conditions and skiing fast, where anything that helps reduce vibration is a bonus. Flexing mode is useful when skiing in soft and deep snow where vibration is not such a problem and a uniform flex is more important, however, the differences are small.

EASE OF USE

'Step in' bindings enable you to put your skis on without bending down. You simply step into them and they close under your body's weight.

Bindings that can be opened with a ski pole enable you to take your skis off without bending down.

Both of these features are useful and practical.

Lifter Plates

Lifter plates raise your boot above the ski. Lifter plates offer three advantages:
1. The extra height gives you more leverage, helping you to tilt your skis. This gives you more power to set an edge, and makes the ski more sensitive.
2. They give more clearance between the snow and the side of the boot when skiing very steep slopes.
3. They dampen vibration (some types only).
  One disadvantage of lifter plates is the weight they add to the ski.
  One concern regarding lifter plates is that they may cause additional strain to the leg, which may cause injury. Guidelines may be introduced to suggest maximum advised levels that the binding should be raised.

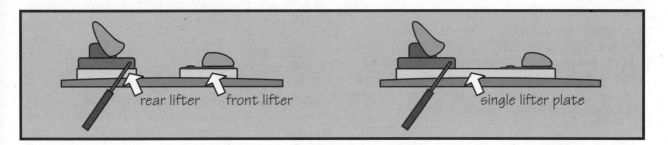

rear lifter   front lifter   single lifter plate

OPTIONS
Lifter plates are available as:
1. A separate product that fits between the binding and the ski. You must ensure that these plates are compatible with your current bindings. Also check that your ski brakes are long enough to stop your skis. They may need to be longer due to the extra height of the binding above the ski; check with ski shop staff. There are two types:
a) With two separate parts for each ski, one to sit under the toepiece and the other under the heelpiece.
b) With one plate for each ski, to sit under the whole length of the binding.
2. An integral part of the binding. These bindings may come as a separate toe and heelpiece or as one piece.

TILTED LIFTER PLATES
Using tilted lifter plates, equipment designers have the potential to design boots with less ramp angle and forward lean. This should result in ski boots that are easier to walk in, once suitable binding release mechanisms can be designed for use with higher lifters. Keep your fingers crossed for the future.

Poles

Poles should be light and strong. The lighter and stronger the better.

ALUMINIUM POLES

Different grades of aluminium alloy have different strength to weight ratios. Lighter poles can be stronger than heavier poles if they are made from a better quality alloy. Some poles bend under load, others snap. I prefer ones that bend as they can often be bent back.

COMPOSITE POLES

Composite poles made from Kevlar and carbon fibres are strong and light.

Some models tend to vibrate when planted, which can feel less secure. You can check this in the ski shop with a few trial plants on the carpet. Compare the effect with aluminium poles.

TIPS OF POLES

I prefer ski poles that have small diameter tips. These grip well in icy conditions. They should be made of hardened steel for durability.

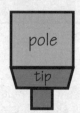

BASKET SIZE

A standard size basket of around 9 cm diameter is a practical size.

For skiing on firm snow, or in bumps, smaller diameter baskets are available. These are more suited to ski competitors who don't want a larger basket that may deflect the pole before the tip bites in.

Although small baskets are suited to firm snow, they are useless in powder because they sink in and give little support.

POLE LENGTH

The standard method used to choose pole length is to turn the pole upside down and hold it below the basket. When your upper arm is **vertical**, your lower arm should be **horizontal**.

I find that poles chosen this way are too long. Instead I do the same test holding the pole the right way up and gripping the handle as normal. This gives a shorter length, which is often preferred by bump skiers.

Poles that are too long force you to ski with your upper body too upright. This forces your weight back onto the tails of your skis. Poles of the right length enable you to position your weight forward.

Borrowing different size poles can be enlightening, especially if you have always skied with poles that are too long. It may take you a few runs to get accustomed to the different length because they can feel quite different.

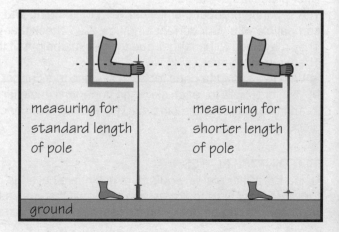

measuring for standard length of pole

measuring for shorter length of pole

ground

Functional Clothing

There is a wide range of clothing that is fashionable and functional. But some ski clothing is fashionable rather than functional, so doesn't keep you warm or dry. The wrong clothing impairs your performance and puts you at risk from the weather.

BODY TEMPERATURE

Your body has to maintain a working temperature of 37+/-0.5 degrees Celsius. If your body temperature drops by half a degree, your decision making and competence will start to be affected. If your core temperature drops to 35 degrees, you will be in a life-threatening situation and classified as hypothermic. Your decision-making skills will have long gone.

TEMPERATURE CONTROL

Your body produces heat from chemical reactions within the cells.

Your body has three ways to regulate its temperature:

1. Varying the flow of blood to the skin: Reducing blood flow to the skin is your body's way of keeping your core (head and torso) warm. Extremities (hands and feet) feel colder when this happens, as less blood flows to them. This makes them more susceptible to cold damage such as frost bite.

2. Producing sweat: This allows the body to cool down. Heat from the body is used to evaporate the sweat on the skin. The heat needed to change the liquid sweat into water vapour (gas) is called the latent heat of evaporation.

3. Shivering: This muscle movement creates heat.

Your body's thermostat for regulating temperature can only work in a limited range of conditions; outside of that range you need suitable clothing.

ENVIRONMENT

The environment affects your body temperature in three ways as you ski.

Conduction: Body heat is lost to the surrounding air. Air is fortunately a good insulator, which is why we can survive in cold climates. Heat is also lost through the soles of your feet.

Convection: Heat is lost through air passing over you (wind-chill). Wind can quickly wick away your body heat. The rate of loss is dependent on air temperature and wind velocity. When you ski, you create wind-chill as you move through the air.

Radiation: While radiation can be responsible for your body overheating, it doesn't cool you to any great degree. Silver coatings (used to reflect radiation) on garments are therefore not that effective in keeping you warm.

FOOD & DRINK IS YOUR FUEL

Food and drink is the **fuel** that enables your body to create heat. In cold weather you need to increase your food intake because you burn more calories to keep warm. Skiing also burns additional calories, as your body is exercising. You may notice that you feel more hungry than usual.

I like to eat a hot high calorie breakfast with several hot drinks in the morning before skiing. During the day I do not eat a large meal as I am exercising. Instead I have a couple of substantial snacks with hot drinks.

Multi-Layer System

An effective way to keep warm is to wear multiple layers of thin insulating clothing rather than a few thick layers. This method of insulation is used by mountaineers and people working in cold places such as Antarctica. Having multiple layers allows you to easily regulate your body temperature by adding or removing layers. Multi-layer clothing systems are also multifunctional as the layers can be used for other activities.

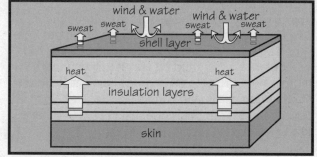

CLOTHING

Your clothing should do three things.

1. Insulate you: Clothing surrounds you with a layer of insulation that slows down the rate that your body loses heat. It is not just the fabric itself that keeps you warm, but the still air that is trapped within it and between the layers.

2. Keep the wind out: For the insulating layers to be effective, you have to have a still air environment, with no wind.

3. Keep you dry: Water is one of the worst insulators. If the insulating layers become wet, water replaces the insulating air in the clothing, making it less effective against the cold.

UPPER BODY LAYERS

I use up to five layers for my upper body depending on temperature.

1. Polypropylene vest, long-sleeved.
2. Polypropylene vest, short-sleeved.
3. Fleece pullover.
4. Zip-up fleece or fibre-pile jacket.
5. Breathable shell jacket.

LOWER BODY LAYERS

I use less insulation for my legs as they are active when skiing and can become too hot.

1. Polypropylene long johns (seldom needed).
2. Fleece trousers.
3. Breathable shell trousers.

SHELL LAYER (WIND/RAIN PROTECTION)

The shell layer is the outermost layer. Breathable waterproof fabrics make ideal shell layers because they keep rain, snow and wind out, yet still allow water vapour (sweat) to escape.

Non-breathable fabrics, while keeping the elements out, trap body moisture. This creates a humid environment that feels clammy.

Having a shell layer that is not insulated makes it more versatile. You can use it in the springtime with only a few layers underneath, or in the heart of winter with many layers (if it is big enough).

Separate jacket and trousers are more versatile and practical than a one-piece ski suit as the items can be used independently and for different activities.

When buying shell clothing, ensure that all seams are tape sealed. If the stitched seams are not sealed, they will leak. It is easy to check an unlined jacket as you can see the tape on the inside seams.

Extremities

MORE INFO

Extremities are usually the first to feel the cold and suffer from any cold damage such as frost nip or, more seriously, frostbite (read page 158 for information on these).

HATS
I find fleece hats most effective. If they have a shell layer over the top, all the better. Many hats do not fully cover the lobe of the ear, which puts the ear at risk of frostbite.

SOCKS
I prefer loop-stitched socks because their smooth shape gives greater comfort. Ribbed socks can press into the foot. Socks should come above the cuff of your boots, so they do not form an uncomfortable ridge where they finish.

Two pairs are warmer than one, provided that adding an extra pair will not crush your toes against the end of the boots and limit circulation. I always ski with two pairs. Note that if you start using two pairs, your boots may feel sloppy if you go back to wearing one pair. When buying boots, fit to one pair as the inner boot will pack down.

MITTS AND GLOVES
Good quality mitts always give better insulation than gloves, but it is harder to do things when wearing mitts. For this reason, I use normal skiers' gloves when I can and mountaineering mitts when it's colder. The mitts I use have a thick fibre-pile inner (multi-layer fleece is also good) with outers made from a breathable waterproof fabric, reinforced in the palm and thumb for additional wear and grip. This type of mitt is usually found in mountaineering shops rather than ski shops. Some snowboarding gloves and mitts are really well designed and suitable for skiing too.

NECKWARMERS
Neckwarmers win hands down over scarves because they stay in place and don't have cold spots. I like a really long design that is twice the standard length and made from fleece. When a storm comes in, I can pull it over my mouth and lower face, while still leaving my neck covered.

I make my own from a fifty centimetre square piece of fleece folded in half. Fleece doesn't fray so you only have to sew one seam along the edge.

Fleece is available with a two-way stretch, but is more commonly found with stretch in one direction. When sewing this type ensure that the stretch is around the tube, so the fabric stretches as you pull it over your head.

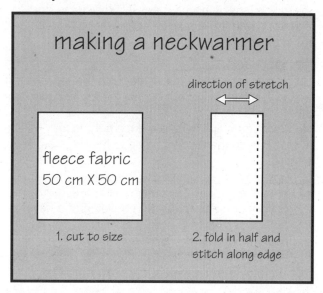

making a neckwarmer

direction of stretch

fleece fabric
50 cm X 50 cm

1. cut to size

2. fold in half and stitch along edge

Sunglasses & Goggles

Sunglasses and goggles are needed when skiing to give protection from the sun's rays. Snow, being white, reflects the sun's rays and subjects you to more light than usual. Even on a cloudy day, the damaging rays can be intense as they bounce back and forth between the clouds and the snow. Choose sunglasses and goggles that protect against ultra violet (UV) light rays.

SUNGLASSES
Sunglasses are more comfortable than goggles on a sunny day. If you are skiing fast the wind can make your eyes water. Wraparound sunglasses keep the wind out of your eyes better than ordinary sunglasses.

GOGGLES
When it starts to snow you need to use goggles because snow gets behind the lenses of sunglasses, making it difficult to see. Goggles should fit on your head tightly, so they don't come off in a fall. Once goggles come off, snow gets on the inside lens. If this happens it is difficult to dry them out, and they usually fog up when you put them back on.

HARD OR SOFT LENSES?
I always used to crack hard goggle lenses down the middle, just above the nose. Now, by using soft lens goggles, I avoid the problem. However, soft lens goggles may be more prone to scratching.

WHAT COLOUR LENSES?
When the sky is cloudy, it can be hard to see the ups and downs of the snow's surface. This is called flat light. In flat light some lens colours allow you to see better than others. I prefer orange lenses, but pink lenses are good too. I prefer a very pale lens in goggles, which are often used when conditions are dull. I use a darker lens in sunglasses.

FOGGED GOGGLES
So far I've not found a pair of goggles that doesn't fog up. In dry conditions some are O.K, but when things become a little damp, out comes the fog. Double lenses are the only choice if you want to see anything at all.
Here are some tips to help reduce goggle fog:
1. Don't touch the inside surface of the goggles. This is easier said than done, especially when you can't see a thing.
2. Apply an anti-fog coating to the inside lens, but this means touching it. I try not to touch the inside lens when it's new, but as it becomes older I resort to coating it.
3. Put your goggles on inside a building and never take them off outside when it is damp. This keeps the inside lens dry.
4. Ensure the air-vents are clear of snow.
5. Keep moving so air flows through the vents. If you are standing still and your goggles fog try fanning air into them by moving them on and off your face.

This chapter explains how to repair and tune up your ski equipment.

Well-tuned skis are a joy to ski, giving better glide for easier and less tiring skiing.

The bases should be flat, the edges sharp, and the bases coated with wax.

Having the right tools for the job makes lighter work of ski maintenance. Many people buy tools as they need them, thereby building up a toolbox over time. Items marked * are optional.

TOOLS

General: bench; vice (ideally a proper ski-repair vice); tip & tail supports (when in the vice); short piece of shock cord (to hold up ski brakes); *apron; lint-free rags; file block and tiny G-clamp.

Repair tools: no 2 & 3 Pozidrive screwdriver; medium & large screwdriver; hand, battery or power drill; 3.5 mm to 4.1 mm drills; countersink tool; *thread tap; *tap wrench; scriber; finger drill or centre punch; ruler; tape measure; hobby knife; *chisel; pliers; hacksaw; hammer; 2 medium-sized G-clamps; *patch template; plumb line; fibre-tip pen; scissors.

Ski-tuning tools: cabinet maker's metal scraper; true bar (any straight edge); Pansar (car body) file; medium & coarse double-cut 25 cm flat files; *coarse double-cut 25 cm three square (triangle) file; *strip of aluminium to clean files; *base planing tool; diamond stone; *toothbrush to clean diamond stone; *rilling tool; Scotchbrite pad; silicon carbide paper (various grit sizes); household iron; stiff-haired nylon brush; * soft-haired brush; felt-tip pen; cigarette lighter; *edge bevel protractor; cork block or felt pad.

MATERIALS

P-tex wire or ribbon or rod; *household candle; base patch material; variety of waxes; plastic hole plugs; helicoils; waterproof woodworking adhesive; two-part slow-set epoxy resin adhesive; masking tape; duct tape; electrical tape; *edge screws; self-adhesive boot padding.

MAKING A FILE-BLOCK

A file-block is simply a piece of wood 35 mm x 35 mm x 200 mm with the corners rounded off. Though simple to make, it is the most effective edge-filing guide I have used and is the cheapest. To use it as a file guide, clamp a flat file to it with a tiny G-clamp. This system may look cumbersome, but is easy to hold. It enables you to:

a) File ski side edges at a uniform angle, with or without edge bevel.

b) Pivot the file so you can file under the binding, which gets in the way when filing side edges.

c) Cut with different parts of the file, so you can spread the wear over the length of the file.

d) Pivot the file so it sits at the correct angle to cut most effectively.

It is also useful for many other jobs:

1. A sanding block for levelling bases.
2. A sanding block for structuring bases.
3. Scraper support to stop scraper bowing.
4. Filing tool for sharpening scraper.
5. Clamping block when gluing ski repairs.

Note: Use a pad to protect file from damage by the G-clamp.

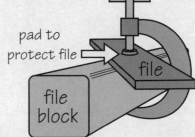

pad to protect file

file

file block

ALL FILES ARE NOT CREATED EQUAL

Ski edges are made from hardened steel, which quickly blunts some files. While many files are made from a very hard material having a high hardness rating, it is the better quality (and usually more expensive) files made from **alloy steel** rather than **carbon steel** that last longer.

Remember to clean files regularly with a thin strip of aluminium.

IRONS

Special hot-waxing irons are available, but many people use an old household clothes iron. If you choose to use a clothes iron, ensure that it isn't a steam iron because of holes in the base where wax can run. Don't use the iron for clothes after working on skis.

ADHESIVES

1. For base patches, edge and sidewall repairs, use two-part epoxy resin adhesive. Specialist epoxy resins for this type of work are available from ski shops, and general-use epoxy resins are available from hardware stores. Check the minimum working temperature. They shouldn't become **brittle** when cold, otherwise they may crack in use due to the constant flexing of the ski. General-use epoxy resins are available as **slow-set** or **quick-set**, I've found that repairs with the quick-set type quickly fail. The slow-set type sets in twelve hours and gains full strength after two or three days. For an urgent repair, find out if a ski shop has facilities to heat up the repair, to cure the adhesive more quickly.
2. For binding screws, use a **waterproof** woodworking adhesive, so screws can be removed.

METAL CABINET MAKER'S SCRAPER

A scraper is a key tool for repairing skis. It can be used with a **sharp** edge to scrape down base material, and with a **dull** edge to scrape off ski wax. If you keep one edge sharp and the other dull, one scraper will do both jobs. Mark the scraper with a file nick, so you know which edge is which.

A new scraper is not sharp, and may not be straight along either edge. To prepare the scraper:
1. File both edges level. When filing, keep the file over the whole length of the scraper, keep it level, and use even pressure. Use a file block to prevent the file rocking.
2. Use a diamond stone to lightly deburr edges.
3. To create a dull edge use a diamond stone.
4. To create a sharp edge you must make a burr along the edge. It is the burr that does the cutting. You could use the burr created by the file. But a better way is to bow the scraper and run the shaft of a large screwdriver along the edge a few times. This gives a sharp uniform burr. This technique may take a little practise. When edge becomes blunt use your screwdriver shaft to create a new burr. Occasionally file edges to level them up.

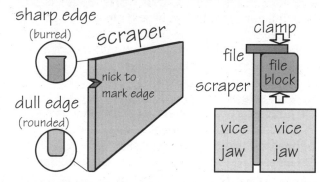

Safety

Maintaining and tuning ski equipment involves working with potentially hazardous materials and machines. While manufacturers may give (in their estimation) safe working guidelines, what is regarded as safe today is sometimes found to be hazardous tomorrow.

I am not able to comment on safe usage of particular products. However, I can bring your attention to some of the hazards that I am aware of, and leave you with the impression that there are almost certainly others. I suggest that you ask manufacturers for safe working guidelines for their products.

SOME HAZARDS

Vapours: heating up waxes, ski base repair materials and ski bases creates vapours that may be dangerous if breathed. If some ski waxes are heated above the recommended temperature, they produce a highly poisonous gas. Hazards can be avoided by not exposing **solid** waxes, **liquid** waxes or wax **vapours** to naked flames, cigarettes (being smoked or left burning in an ash tray), electric irons turned up too high, heat guns (as used in commercial ski-repair workshops), some types of room heaters and similar appliances. If cigarettes, unlit or lit, are **touched** with wax-coated hands, wax will be transferred to the cigarette. If smoked, dangerous fumes from the wax will be given off and inhaled.

Solvents may give off poisonous fumes. If left on cleaning rags, the solvent will evaporate into the work area. This can be avoided by putting solvent-soaked rags in an appropriately labelled airtight container.

Use suitable vapour-protection masks if working indoors. A ventilated area with extraction fans and a supply of clean air improves working conditions.

Dust: sanding ski bases, ski base repair materials, and wax creates dust. Breathing dust cannot be regarded as safe. Use a dust mask.

Electricity: unprotected light bulbs may be knocked by skis and break, giving an electric shock to the person holding the skis. Remember that skis have steel edges running down their length that conduct electricity. Protect light bulbs in workshop areas.

Fire: hot irons, naked flames and other sources of heat present fire hazards. Most solvents are highly flammable. A lighted P-tex candle may drip P-tex material that remains alight. Floor materials are sometimes made from flammable materials or may be covered with flammable debris or dust.

Machinery: power tools can cause eye damage and catch hold of loose hair. Use suitable eye protection and wear a hat to cover hair.

Sprays: sprays can cause eye damage. Use suitable eye protection.

Liquids: splashes of liquids, such as solvents (especially if hot) can easily cause eye damage. Use suitable eye protection. Solvents can cause skin irritation, so avoid skin contact.

Adhesives: avoid contact with skin.

Ski edges: burrs on ski edges can easily cut hands. Burrs can be removed easily with a diamond stone.

Ski Maintenance

Skis may have to be repaired due to damage, or tuned up due to general wear and tear. The following steps show the logical approach.

maintenance sequence

1. edge & sidewall repairs

2. base repairs

3. flattening bases

4. sharpening edges

5. structuring bases

6. waxing bases

Edge & Sidewall Repairs

Skiing over rocks can result in sections of edge being pulled from a ski. If skiing over a rock is inevitable, try to ensure that the skis don't pass over the rock sideways because this will tend to pull the edges out from the skis. It is usually better to let the length of the ski run along the rock. This may create a long scar in the base, but may keep your edges intact and be easier to repair. Use leg retraction if you are about to ski over a rock, to take your weight off your skis.

TOOLS
- Ski vices
- Hobby knife
- Hacksaw
- Pliers
- Chisel
- File block
- G-clamps (medium x2)
- Coarse double-cut 25 cm flat file.
- Felt-tip pen

MATERIALS
- Spare edges
- Two-part slow-set epoxy resin adhesive
- Wax
- Electrical tape
- Edge screws (optional)

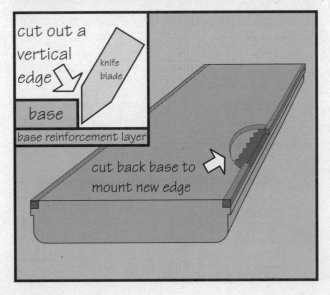

cut out a vertical edge

knife blade

base

base reinforcement layer

cut back base to mount new edge

MAKING AN EDGE REPAIR

1. Expose the glued part of the ski's edge by cutting back the P-tex base where edge is damaged. When cutting back the base, angle the knife blade to cut a vertical edge in the base material. This will help the P-tex (that you will later fill the hole with) to stay in place.
2. Carefully cut out the damaged length of edge with a hacksaw. You only need cut through the square section of the edge; the thin strip behind can be snapped off with pliers. With sectional edges, sawing is not necessary. Just use pliers to break off the damaged sections.
3. Make up a length of edge to fit in the damaged area. Spare sections of edge are available from ski shops, or can be taken from old or broken skis.
4. Level the surface with a chisel, so the new edge can be glued down just proud of the existing edge.
5. Glue the new edge in place. Remember some glue will probably be needed under the ends of the existing edge. Edge screws can be used for added security, but are not necessarily needed.
6. Clamp the edge in place while the glue sets. Applying a coating of wax to clamps and anything used to assist clamping (e.g. file block) ensures that they don't become stuck to the ski by mistake.
7. When the glue has gained full strength, file down the new edge to match the existing edge.
8. Fill the hole in the base with P-tex (see next section) and have the bases ground if necessary.

Edge & Sidewall Repairs

EMERGENCY EDGE REPAIR

This method gives an edge made of resin. There is the risk with this type of repair that more of the edge may pull out of the ski with use. Only use this method on old skis that you don't care about.

1. Expose the glued part of the ski's edge by cutting back the P-tex base where the edge is damaged.
2. Carefully cut out the damaged length of edge.
3. Remove loose debris from the repair area.
4. Roughen the area to help the epoxy resin stick.
5. Place electrical tape along the sidewall of the ski, beside the repair area, to act as a mould.
6. Tilt the base of the ski to 10 degrees, with the damaged side lower.
7. Pour slow-set two-part epoxy resin adhesive into the damaged area and under the ends of the edges.
8. When set, remove the tape. File down the adhesive to the level of the ski base to give the new adhesive edge. File along sidewall if necessary.
9. Fill the rest of the damaged area with P-tex (see next section).

CRACKED EDGES - PROS & CONS

Cracked (sectional) edges have fine cracks at regular intervals (about every 25 mm) along the edge.

I have found that cracked edges are more prone to pulling out of the ski than continuous edges. Sectional edges, however, have the advantage that the original edge can often be glued back in place. This is because the segments, being short, seldom bend when pulled out of the ski. Continuous edges always bend as they pull out, making it impossible to reinsert them.

USE DAMAGED EDGE FOR THE OUTSIDE EDGE

Try to use the repaired edge as an outside edge. Outside edges have lighter use, so the repair is less likely to be pulled out. To achieve this, mark your skis left and right.

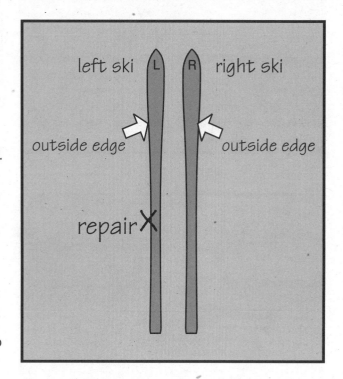

REPAIRING SIDEWALLS

Small areas of damage to sidewalls can be repaired with slow-set two-part epoxy resin adhesive. Duct or electrical tape may be needed to make a mould.

Base Repairs

Skiing over rocks damages ski bases, but repairs are usually straightforward. Small gouges that don't cut into the layer beneath the base may not even need to be repaired, unless you are a racer and need immaculate bases for speed.

TOOLS
- Ski vices
- Hobby knife
- Household iron **or** cigarette lighter
- Patch template
- File block
- Thin strip of wood
- G-clamp (medium x2)
- Pansar file **or** scraper

MATERIALS
- P-tex (4 mm wire, ribbon, rods, **or** candles)
- Base patches
- Household candle
- Two-part slow-set epoxy resin adhesive
- Duct tape
- Wax

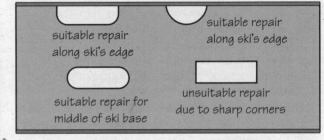

suitable repair along ski's edge

suitable repair along ski's edge

suitable repair for middle of ski base

unsuitable repair due to sharp corners

REPAIRING HOLES BY MELTING IN P-TEX
The damaged area should be dry before repairing.
1. If damage goes through the base material, cut around the damaged area with a hobby knife, until you have a clean-sided cut-out. Curved-shape repairs hold the repair material better than square-cornered shapes. The cut-out should also have a vertical-sided edge to help hold in the repair material. Roughen the floor of the repair area with a knife blade to give better adhesion.
2. Fill the hole by melting in P-tex. Use one of two methods; melting with a household iron or lighting a P-tex candle (see details of both on page 137). Build up the P-tex in layers until it is above the base of the ski. Let the P-tex cool between layers. This helps to prevent the P-tex from **bubbling**. If the P-tex starts to bubble, pull out the repair material and start again.
3. After applying the final layer, let the repair cool. If it's cold outside, put the skis out to speed up cooling.
4. Trim off the excess P-tex with a pansar file or a scraper. If the repair has not thoroughly cooled before you start, it will probably rip out.

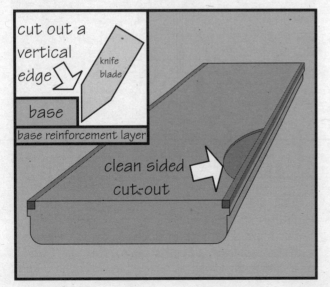

cut out a vertical edge

knife blade

base

base reinforcement layer

clean sided cut-out

Base Repairs

TYPE OF P-TEX

P-tex repair material, like ski bases, is available in various grades, each with its own pros and cons.

When choosing P-tex you may want to consider:
a) Hardness (resistance to rock damage).
b) Durability (resistance to snow abrasion).
c) Adherence properties (to ski base material).
d) Adherence properties (to layer beneath ski base).
e) Adherence properties (to ski edges).

Different types suit different tasks and skis. Ski shop staff can advise you on the different P-tex materials available.

IRONING P-TEX & CANDLE-BURNING P-TEX

Using an electric iron to melt P-tex can give good results. If you use the same iron for hot-waxing, ensure the iron is clean of wax. An iron used for ski work **cannot be used for clothes**.

P-tex candles burn and the melted material is run into the repair. This method deposits **black soot**, which gives an unprofessional-looking repair. This technique is more suited for temporary repairs, when an iron isn't available.

To reduce soot as much as possible: keep the repair candle burning with a blue rather than a yellow flame; let the P-tex run in one continual stream rather than dripping it into the repair; keep the repair candle close to the base; start by letting the p-tex run onto a metal scraper on the base before running it into the repair.

A short lighted household candle nearby is useful to re-light the repair candle when it goes out.

Drips from the repair candle are often **alight** and therefore a **fire hazard**. Be careful where it drips.

REPAIRING HOLES BY P-TEX PATCHING

Patching is a particularly useful technique for larger repairs that go through the base material.

The damaged area should be dry before repairing.
1. Cut out a patch and a matching shape over the repair in the ski base. Cut the patch with rounded rather than square corners (square-cornered patches are more prone to pulling out in use). Cut the patch and cut-out with vertical edges (for a better fit). To assist cutting, use a patch-cutting template.
2. Roughen the base of the repair and one side of the patch. Clean away loose particles and dust.
3. Glue together and place a strip of duct tape over the top of the repair. Put a waxed (so it doesn't stick) file block over the tape. Put a strip of wood on the top sheet of the ski (so the clamp doesn't damage it) and clamp the whole lot together with even pressure.
4. After the resin has set, level the repair with a pansar file or scraper. Fill any gaps by melting in P-tex.
5. Level again with a pansar file or scraper.

patch template

DELAMINATIONS

Delaminations are where layers of the ski separate, usually at the tip or tail of the ski. To repair:
1. Dry out the ski thoroughly.
2. Remove loose material.
3. Glue, then clamp delaminated parts together with even pressure. Use strips of wood to spread the clamping load and avoid damage to skis. Wax the clamps etc so they don't adhere to the ski.

Flattening Bases

Ski bases must be kept flat otherwise the skis become difficult to control.

CHECKING FLATNESS

Check for flatness by running a true bar (straight edge) along the whole length of the ski's base. Look for any light shining through gaps between the ski and the true bar. A flat ski has no gaps.

EFFECTS OF SHAPE ON PERFORMANCE

Skis can either be flat, base-high, edge-high or railed. The shape of the base affects the way your skis handle.

Flat: a flat base is the ideal. The ski feels stable in a straight line, and tracks well.

Base-high: a base-high ski has its base proud of the edges. Base-high skis feel unstable. They tend to float at the tip and tail, and don't track well in a straight line.

Edge-high or railed: an edge-high or railed-edge ski has its edges proud of the base. These skis 'catch edges' when skiing in a straight line and hook unpredictably in the snow, making skiing difficult.

MACHINING BASES

Ski bases can be kept flat by hand-filing, if you are enthusiastic enough. New technology has resulted in harder bases that are more durable and resistant to abrasion, but harder to file, sand, or plane flat. Skis that have not been regularly maintained and are edge or base-high can be difficult to level by hand. The easiest and most practical way is to take your skis to a ski shop for stone-grinding or belt-sanding by machine.

These techniques level the base and structure it for you (see page 143 for details on structuring).

true bar

flat ski

base high ski

edge high ski

railed edge ski

Flattening Bases

MORE INFO

TOOLS
- Vice
- Ski brake retainer
- Coarse double-cut 25 cm flat **or** 3 square (triangle) file
- Coarse silicon carbide paper and a file block **or** scraper **or** base-planing tool
- Diamond stone

LEVELLING EDGE-HIGH SKIS BY HAND
Before filing edges read the work hardening note on this page.

Skis that are slightly edge high or have railed edges can be levelled by hand, using a coarse double-cut 25 cm flat or three square (triangle) file. Triangle files are useful because their shape gives the file rigidity; being narrower, more pressure can be applied to any one area at a time. Both edges are filed together to help ensure flatness. To prevent filings impregnating the base, brush them away regularly.

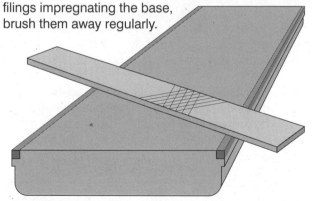

LEVELLING BASE-HIGH SKIS BY HAND
If skis are only slightly base high they can be levelled by hand.

There are three ways to do this:
1. Use coarse silicone carbide paper around a file block to sand down the base.
2. Use a sharp metal scraper to scrape the base down. Ensure that your thumbs do not flex the scraper. To prevent this, you can put a file block behind the scraper.
3. Use a base-planing tool.

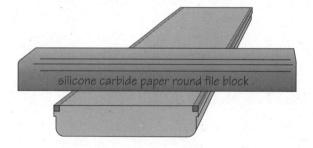

silicone carbide paper round file block

WORK HARDENED EDGES
If a ski's edge runs over a rock, the surface layer of the metal edge may be scored and marked, giving a glazed appearance. This distortion of the metal makes it harder on the surface. The process is know as **work hardening**.

Before filing, check ski edges for signs of rock damage. Most damage usually occurs directly under the binding because the skier weight applies greater pressure to this area. The hardened layer can be removed with a diamond stone. Removing the hardened layer prevents damage to files.

Sharpening Edges

A standard edge has one face parallel with the base, and the other perpendicular (90 degrees) to it. Any modifications to this results in a bevelled edge. Bevelling can enhance the performance of your skis. Racers may bevel their edges to suit the snow conditions of a particular race. While this gives high performance, changing the angle of bevel diminishes the ski's edges, and thereby the life of the ski. For this reason, recreational skiers tend to find edge angles that suit them, and then stick with them.

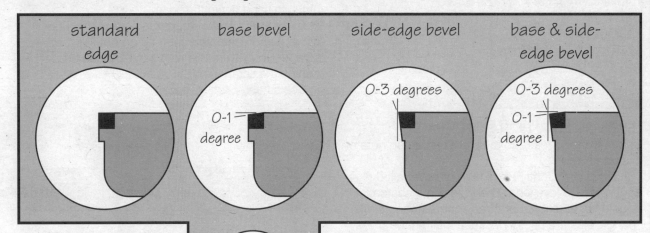

standard edge base bevel side-edge bevel base & side-edge bevel

0-1 degree

0-3 degrees

0-3 degrees

0-1 degree

recessed edge

RECESSED EDGES

The stone-grinding process may recess the ski edges by a fraction of a millimetre. This can happen because the polyethylene base compresses under the grinding process, then recovers afterward. If your edges have been recessed by stone grinding, you may not want to base-bevel your skis. This is because a recessed edge has similar characteristics to a base-bevelled edge.

Note that it isn't possible to recess edges by hand-tuning techniques.

PROS & CONS OF BASE-BEVELLING

Skis are easier to turn if base-bevelled, and their edges catch less. Racers use base-bevelling to reduce edge drag, so they can ski faster. But base-bevelling increases the edge angle, so the edge is less sharp. In soft snow this doesn't matter, and may be desirable, but on ice, grip is sacrificed.

PROS & CONS OF SIDE-EDGE BEVELLING

Skis with side-edge bevelling have better grip. This is particularly useful when skiing on firm or icy slopes, but can make the ski grab in softer snow.

Side-edge bevelling complements base-bevelling by providing a sharper edge angle to a base-bevelled edge.

Sharpening Edges

MORE INFO

HOW MUCH BEVEL

When deciding on the amount of bevel, both the base and side edges have to be considered together because their combined values determine the final edge angle of the ski.

One approach is to first decide how much base-edge bevel you want, and then decide on how sharp you want your edges to be. Once you know this, you can use the right amount of side-edge bevel to suit.

The base bevel for recreational skiing should range from zero to one degree.

Sharper edge angles give better extra grip on harder snow; more oblique angles are better for softer snow so the skis don't grab. 87 degrees is suitable for ice and 91 degrees for soft snow.

Here are some examples of bevelling combinations:

1 deg base + 0 deg side = 91 deg edge
0 deg base + 0 deg side = 90 deg edge
1 deg base + 1 deg side = 90 deg edge
0 deg base + 1 deg side = 89 deg edge
1 deg base + 2 deg side = 89 deg edge
0 deg base + 2 deg side = 88 deg edge
1 deg base + 3 deg side = 88 deg edge
0 deg base + 3 deg side = 87 deg edge

For all-purpose use, try a half degree of base bevel and an edge angle of 89 degrees. This gives one and a half degrees of side-edge bevel.

PROGRESSIVE BEVELLING

Some ski racers use different amounts of base or side-edge bevel along the length of the ski, and some bevel the inside and outside edges differently.

TOOLS	MATERIALS
- Ski vices	- Masking tape
- Ski brake retainer	
- Felt-tip pen	
- Edge bevel protractor	
- Coarse 25 cm flat file	
- Filing block	
- G-clamp (tiny)	
- Pansar file	
- Diamond stone	

HOW TO SHARPEN/BEVEL THE BASE EDGES

1. Remove any work-hardened (see page 139) surfaces with a diamond stone.
2. File edges one at a time, using a file with masking tape wrapped around one end to tilt the file to the desired angle (measure with edge bevel protractor). Marking the edges with a felt-tip pen before filing helps you to see how your filing is progressing.
3. Polish base edges with a diamond stone. The extent you polish depends on whether you are a racer or recreational skier.

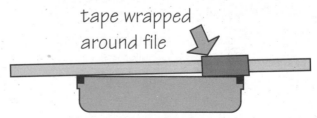

tape wrapped around file

Sharpening Edges

HOW TO SHARPEN/BEVEL THE SIDE EDGES

1. When sharpening/bevelling side edges, some sidewall material may first have to be removed with a pansar file.

2. File edges using a file and file block secured with a G-clamp. The angle can be set by applying masking tape to the corner of the file block (measure with edge bevel protractor). Before filing, mark along the edges with a felt-tip pen so you can monitor the amount of filing.

3. Filing causes a burr along the edge. Remove this with a diamond stone.

4. Polish side edges with a diamond stone.

5. De-tune (dull) the tip and tail by lightly running a diamond stone over the edge.
 Note side edges can be sharpened by machine.

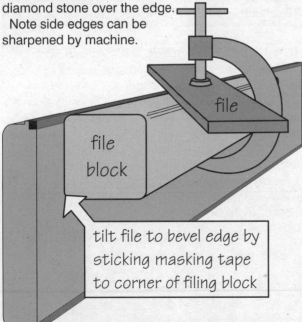

file

file block

tilt file to bevel edge by sticking masking tape to corner of filing block

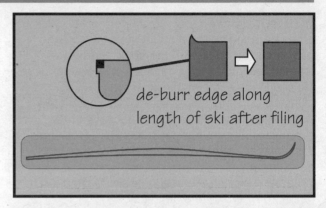

de-burr edge along length of ski after filing

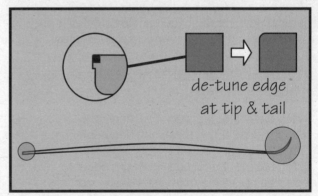

de-tune edge at tip & tail

RE-SHARPENING EDGES

Once skis have been bevelled, the edges should be kept sharp. Re-sharpen the side edges more frequently than the base edges to prevent the ski becoming base high so soon.

DEBURR TAIL-GUARD

Skiing causes burrs to build up on the aluminium tail-guard on the end of the skis. These burrs can be removed with a file.

Structuring Bases

Structuring puts grooves into the base of your skis to improve glide and ease of turning.

SIZE OF STRUCTURED GROOVES

Fine structure: use for cold dry snow.
Coarse structure: use for warm wet snow.

Fine structure reduces friction in cold and dry snow. When the snow becomes wet, e.g. in spring, the high water content results in **suction** between the ski and the snow. A coarser structure is thought to channel away the water more effectively, in a similar way to the tread on a car tyre.

STRUCTURING BY MACHINE

When the base of a ski is stone-ground or belt-sanded, the process leaves a structured base. Belt sanders leave a linear structure along the length of the ski while stone grinders can be set to leave various patterns e.g. crosshatch.

linear   crosshatch

STRUCTURING WITH A RILLING TOOL

Rilling rolls (rather than cuts) grooves into the base. Unlike cutting, rolling doesn't remove material, but deforms it. This has the advantage of pulling up minimal hair-like strands from the base. Other techniques pull up a lot of hair-like strands which are difficult to remove. Rilled structures are, however, less permanent than cut structures, and may diminish when heated e.g. by hot waxing. Also, rilling doesn't remove any of the oxidised layer from the base surface (see page 146 for information on oxidisation), whereas cutting techniques do.

Fine- and coarse-grooved rilling tools are available.

TOOLS
- Ski vices
- Ski brake retainer
- Rilling tool **or** silicon carbide paper
- File block
- Scraper
- Scotchbrite pad

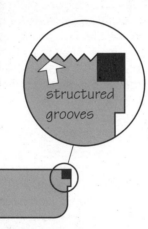

structured grooves

STRUCTURING WITH SILICON CARBIDE PAPER

Using silicon carbide paper structures a base effectively, but fine hairs are pulled up from the base. These are troublesome to remove completely (see section below).

To structure a ski base wrap silicon carbide paper around a file block, for uniform sanding of the base. Sweep away any dust from the base.

REMOVING BASE HAIRS

All structuring techniques leave fine hairs on the surface of the ski. These should be removed before waxing by lightly scraping the structured base with a sharp scraper. Then use a Scotchbrite pad on a file block to rub down the base in both directions, until the hairs have gone.

Waxing Bases

MORE INFO

Waxing skis can be a five-minute process using a simple method of application and a one-wax-does-all (universal wax) approach. Or it can be a complex process where waxes are carefully matched to the snow conditions.

BENEFITS OF WAXING

Wax on skis gives them more glide. More glide enables your skis to go faster and turn more easily, with obvious advantages for racers. It also means that skiing for recreation is **easier** and **less tiring**. For recreational skiers there are additional, more subtle, benefits e.g. when traversing flat sections of the mountain, it takes less effort to push yourself along with your poles. When traversing a slope, it's easier to maintain height because you have more speed. When skiing powder on shallow slopes, the extra glide keeps your speed up where you might otherwise be hardly moving.

CHOOSING A WAX

There is not one wax that offers the best glide in all snow conditions. When waxing for performance, waxes are chosen to match the snow conditions. There are three main considerations in choosing a wax.

1. **Chemical group:** governed by snow conditions and affordability.
2. **Temperature range:** temperature is used to indicate snow condition.
3. **Method of application:** wax is available in different forms: pastes, creams, bars and powders. Each suits different application methods.

chemical group	temperature range	method of application
Current waxes are based on fluorocarbons and hydrocarbons. Fluorocarbon waxes give better glide than hydrocarbon waxes, but are considerably more expensive. Fluorinated waxes are made from a combination of the two chemicals, and bridge the gap in performance and price. Graphite is also added to some waxes.	The temperature of the snowpack is a good indicator of the nature of the snow. Warm snow is wet and .soft. Cold snow is dry and hard. Remember, some companies use air temperature, while others use snow temperature, to describe their waxes. Waxes are available to suit narrow and wide temperature ranges. Racers need waxes to suit specific conditions. Recreational skiers need waxes to suit a broad range of conditions.	**Cold waxing:** Waxes in a solvent are available as a cream or paste. These are rubbed onto the base. When the solvent evaporates, the wax is left behind. Bar wax can also be rubbed directly onto the base. **Hot-waxing:** Hot wax available as a bar is rubbed onto the base and ironed in with a warm iron, or ironed on directly. **Corking:** Powder waxes are sprinkled onto the base (over other waxes), then rubbed in with a cork.

Waxing Bases

PROPERTIES OF SNOW

Snow is in a continual state of transformation. At any moment, surface snow is dependent upon its original state and the changes it has undergone: through heat exchange (via conduction, convection and radiation) and through mechanical effects (skier compaction, wind, snow-grooming). Heat from or to the surface snow is affected by:

Weather: air-snow-ground temperature, wind speed, humidity, cloud cover, reflection.
Location: latitude, altitude, slope aspect, slope angle, snow depth, vegetation.
Time: time of year and day.
Contamination: dust, vegetation debris.

PROPERTIES OF WAXES

Waxes must possess a number of properties (see table below). Generally, soft waxes have a lower coefficient of friction and greater hydrophobicity than harder waxes, but soft waxes have low resistance to snow and dirt impregnation (both can slow down skis by causing drag) and are not as durable as harder waxes.

Additives are used to harden up some waxes to increase durability and resistant to impregnation. This makes them suitable for hard (cold), sharp (new) and dirty (old) snow. Although harder waxes have less hydrophobicity, this is not so important when the snow is cold as there is not much free water in the snowpack.

	snow properties
temp	**dry/wet:** warm snow is wetter than cold snow. Wet snow creates suction between the snow & the skis. This decreases glide. **hard/soft:** cold snow is harder than warm snow and more abrasive to wax.
age	**sharp/rounded:** new snow is sharp while older snow becomes rounded. Artificial snow tends to be sharp and abrasive, which causes wear (base burn). **clean/dirty:** fresh snow is clean whereas older snow becomes dirty.

wax properties
coefficient of friction: wax should have as low a coefficient of friction as possible.
hydrophobicity: wax should repel water to reduce suction, particularly when snow is wet (warm).
durability: the wax must be resistant to abrasion from the snow, particularly when the snow is hard (cold) and sharp (new or artificial).
resistance to snow impregnation: waxes have to be harder when the snow is harder (cold) and sharp (new or artificial) to prevent impregnation.
resistance to dirt impregnation: to avoid drag, the wax must be hard enough to prevent dirt clinging to the base.

Waxing Bases

WAXING FOR RECREATIONAL SKIING

For recreational skiing, speed is not an issue. All that is needed is reasonable glide. So a suitable wax may be a 'one-wax-does-all' (universal wax). Another solution is to choose one of two waxes: a hard wax for cold snow and a soft wax for warm snow.

WAXING FOR PERFORMANCE

Racers wax skis to win races. They use specialist waxes that give optimum glide over a fairly **narrow range** of conditions. It is therefore important that they choose the right wax for a race. To accurately judge the wax needed, they must understand the exact condition of the snow and be able to predict how the weather will affect the snow before the race. This demands an in-depth knowledge of the waxes they use, built up over time from experience and observations.

   Racers are concerned with more than snow temperature when choosing a wax. They bear in mind all the conditions that affect snow (see the previous page) to determine the degree of wetness, hardness, sharpness and cleanliness.

WAXING FOR SPEED RANGE

Skis travelling fast over the snow generate more heat than skis travelling slowly. Because of this, a racer in a fast event (downhill race) might choose a wax suitable for warmer snow conditions than a racer waxing for a slower event (slalom race).

WAXING SIDEWALLS

Racers find it worthwhile to wax the sidewalls of their skis to reduce friction further.

WAX FOR STORAGE

Ski bases should be kept waxed to prevent oxidisation of the base material. Some bases cannot absorb wax so readily if they become oxidised. The oxidised layer can be removed by sanding, or grinding the base.

   Wax edges (base and sides) to prevent rusting during the summer months.

CROSS COUNTRY WAXING NOTE

Cross country skiers use waxes differently to alpine skiers. Besides using **glide** waxes to increase speed, they also use **grip** waxes so they can run on skis over the flat and up slopes. They apply grip wax under the middle of the skis, and glide wax to the tip and tail.

USING A HOUSEHOLD IRON FOR HOT WAXING

 If using a household iron to hot wax skis, note that once you have put wax on it, **it is useless for clothes**, unless you want a batik design.

   Overheating the wax or ski base may: generate unhealthy vapours from the wax or base, delaminate the ski, reduce the wax absorption properties of the base, cause loss of base structure, reduce the properties of the wax.

   To avoid overheating: keep iron temperature as low as possible, check temperature setting before switching on, let the iron warm up fully before you put wax on it, keep the iron moving, don't iron for too long.

Waxing Bases

TOOLS	MATERIALS
- Ski vices	- Waxes
- Ski brake retainer	- Solvent (optional)
- Cloth, iron, cork block **or** felt pad	
- Scraper	
- Nylon brush (stiff- haired)	
- Soft-haired brush	

PREPARATION TECHNIQUES

Ski bases should be clean and dry before you apply a new layer of wax.

Two ways to clean dirty ski bases are:

1. Hot scrape method:

a) Wipe skis with a cloth to remove grit and dirt.

b) Melt wax onto the base with a warm iron, then iron over base (see caution notes on previous page about using a household iron).

c) While the wax is still warm, scrape off with a scraper (read notes on scrapers, page 131).

d) Repeat b & c several times until bases are clean.

2. Solvent method:

Special cleaning solvents can be used to clean the base if necessary. If solvents are used, the skis must be left to dry thoroughly before waxing.

Remember, ski bases should be dry before you wax them. If you bring cold skis into a warm building, condensation will form on them until they warm up.

HINT FOR RUBBING ON BAR WAXES

Bar wax can be quite hard, especially when cold. Bar wax rubs on more easily if the wax (in a plastic bag) is softened in a cup of warm water.

WAX APPLICATION TECHNIQUES

Base should be structured and clean before waxing. Read notes on scrapers (page 131).

Cold waxing:

Rub it on and leave it

Cream, paste or bar wax is rubbed onto the base and left. This is the simplest method of waxing.

Rub - scrape - brush - polish

a) Rub cream, paste or bar wax onto base.

b) Lightly scrape off excess.

c) With a stiff nylon brush, brush wax from base structure and clean away crumbs left by brushing.

d) Use a soft-haired brush to polish the wax.

Hot Waxing:

Rub - iron - scrape - brush - polish

a) Rub bar wax suitable for hot waxing onto base, or melt wax onto base with an iron.

b) Iron wax into base with iron.

c) Scrape off excess once cooled.

d) With a stiff nylon brush, brush wax out of base structure, so structure is visible. Clean off crumbs left by brushing.

e) Use a soft-haired brush to polish the wax.

Corking:

Sprinkle - cork - brush - polish

This type of wax is applied over other waxes.

a) Sprinkle powder wax onto base.

b) Use a cork block or felt pad to rub wax into base.

c) With a stiff nylon brush, brush wax out of base structure, so structure is visible. Clean off crumbs left by brushing.

d) Use a soft-haired brush to polish the wax.

If your boots hurt, you cannot ski to your full potential, if at all. If your boots hurt, you are less likely to go skiing. If your boots hurt, you are less likely to have fun. When buying boots, don't settle for a pair that are painful. The boots should be comfortable when you leave the shop. However, boots that are comfortable in the shop often become painful when skiing. Some ski shops may offer a commitment, as part of the initial cost, to work on your boots until they are comfortable. Check this is so with the staff before the initial fitting and any commitment to buy. If you have second-hand boots, you will have to pay for the service or do it yourself. It can be worth paying as not only do you get the boots fixed, but you can pick up some tips on boot-fitting for the future.

PINPOINTING THE PAIN
To explain to a boot technician where your boots are causing pain, put the boot on the foot that hurts. Point out on your other (bare) foot where it is hurting.

TOOLS	MATERIALS
- Hobby knife	- Self adhesive boot
- Scissors	padding
- G-clamp	- Duct tape
- Fibre-tip pen	

PADDING BOOTS
If your boots are hurting there are several things that can be done. Placing padding around a pressure point takes the force off the point that hurts. A circular doughnut pad, or strips of padding, are useful. Self-adhesive padding is easy to use, although duct tape is useful for holding padding in place. Duct tape is used by skiers, snowboarders, and climbers to fix just about anything that can be fixed. Some would say that if it can't be fixed with duct tape, it can't be fixed at all!

If you cannot get a satisfactory solution to a boot problem by padding the boot, another option is to tape a pad to you. This is inconvenient as the pad needs to be reapplied each time, but it's worth it if nothing else works.

sore spot
doughnut

COMPRESSING PADDING
One way to ease pain from a sore spot is to reduce the padding by compressing the foam. This can be done with a G-clamp. Squeeze the foam until compressed. The degree of effectiveness depends on the inner material. Some materials flow back to their original shape; others remain compressed. Use in conjunction with padding around areas of pain.

Tweaking Boots

MORE INFO

SHAVING INNER BOOT

Shaving or cutting into inner boots should be done with caution as material cannot be easily replaced. It is very easy to cut into a pair of boots, then realise that what you cut out wasn't causing the problem.

I suggest you ask at a ski shop for a second opinion if you have not modified a boot before, or ask the staff to do it. I always try to solve boot problems by adding material if possible. If adding material doesn't work, you can then think about shaving the inner boot or blowing the shells.

BLOWING THE SHELLS

Ski shops have the facility to heat up the shells and 'blow them out.' This expands a small area of the boot where the pain is. This has the advantage that it does not reduce insulation, as shaving the boot would. This can be important in critical areas that are more likely to feel the cold.

BOOTS THAT ARE TOO SMALL IN VOLUME

Boots that don't have enough volume, or are the wrong shape for your foot, hurt and make skiing intolerable. Pressure points reduce blood circulation, making your feet more susceptible to the cold. Consider blowing the shells. Maybe you will have to buy larger boots.

IF YOUR BOOTS ARE TOO SHORT

If your boots feel too short, and you are not using footbeds, inserting these may pull your toes back just enough to take the pressure off. Footbeds arch the foot, and shorten it. Shaving the toes of the inner boots or blowing the shells are other options.

IF YOUR BOOTS ARE TOO BIG

Boots often become too big with age as the inner boots pack down, enabling your feet to move inside your boots. This results in a loss of performance and may cause sore spots where your feet rub. Footbeds or an extra pair of socks will help to take up space in the boots. If you have footbeds already, make up two flat pads and place one under each existing footbed to take up space.

If your boots are obviously too big, you may need a new pair of boots. But you may be able to solve the problem by replacing the inner boots with custom foam-filled inners.

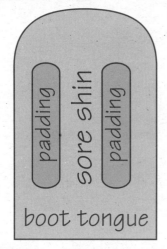

BOOTS THAT GIVE YOU SORE SHINS

If your shin bone is sore, try padding the tongue of the inner boot with strips of padding. Mark where the line of your shin sits against the tongue. You will find that it lies just off centre. Put padding on the outside of the tongue to each side of the shin.

Ski shop technicians can mount bindings in a fraction of the time that you can at home because they use drill jigs (these position the drill). Mounting bindings at home takes time and is prone to errors in hole placement. If you have never mounted bindings before, I suggest practising on an old pair of skis. Because all bindings are different, you will need to use these guidelines in conjunction with your own assessment of what needs to be done for your bindings. If the bindings are supplied with mounting instructions, you may want to use these.

TOOLS
- Ski vices
- Hammer
- Chisel **or** hobby knife
- Fibre-tip pen
- Tape measure
- Ruler
- Scriber
- Finger drill **or** centre punch
- Hand, battery **or** power drill
- Drill bit
- Thread tap for ski-industry type screws
- Tap wrench
- Countersink tool
- Number 3 Pozidrive screwdriver

MATERIALS
- Plastic hole plugs
- Waterproof wood-working adhesive
- Duct tape

PLUGGING OLD HOLES
Use plastic plugs to fill old holes from previously mounted bindings.

Put some waterproof woodworking adhesive in the old hole, then hammer in the plug. If any plastic protrudes, trim off with a chisel or knife.

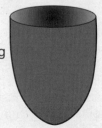

DRILLING AND TAPPING THREADS
To mount bindings, use the drill size recommended for your particular ski. Ski shop staff can tell you this. The size depends on the construction of the ski. It is usually between 3.5 mm and 4.1 mm.

If your skis have a metal top sheet, a thread can be cut with a thread-cutting tap (available from ski shops). If you do not have a tap, the screws can be used to cut their own thread.

TAPE THE DRILL
To prevent drilling deeper than necessary, and to avoid drilling through the base of the ski, wrap tape **securely** around the drill to mark the correct drilling depth.

Note: Tape is prone to sliding along the drill, even when wrapped around tightly.

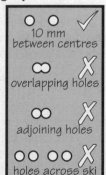

drill

tape

NEIGHBOURING HOLES
When mounting bindings to previously drilled skis, check that new holes will not overlap or adjoin existing holes. Hole centres should be at least 10 mm apart, and further apart if helicoils have been used. Also avoid making a row of holes across the ski, which would weaken it. Make all checks **before drilling any holes**.

O O ✓
10 mm
between centres

∞ ✗
overlapping holes

OO ✗
adjoining holes

OO OO ✗
holes across ski

Mounting Bindings

1. BOOT POSITION ON THE SKI

One theory states that the ball of the foot should be over the centre of the running length. This position is, however, difficult to measure. Manufacturers tend to use other techniques, with the following being widely used:

a) Position the **toe** of the boot on the half chord of the ski.

b) Position the **midpoint** of the boot 15 cm (can vary with ski length) behind the half chord of the ski.

Manufacturers put a mark on the ski (usually on the sidewall) to indicate where either the toe or the midpoint of the boot should be positioned. They don't always indicate which method they are using, so you need to measure the position to check. Don't expect it to be exactly on either of the positions mentioned.

If the ski has no mark, measure the half chord and mount the toe there. To measure the half chord, measure the distance from the tail of the ski to the tip. Divide the length by two. Double this figure to check the calculation. Then mark the halfway position on the ski (with a fibre-tip pen) by measuring from the **tail**. Label the position 'half chord' to avoid any confusion.

Notes:

1. Remember that mounting the binding is always a compromise; there is not a 'right' position, only opinions.

2. Both these methods put the ball of the foot in different positions with different sized boots.

3. The running length in relation to the tip and tail varies. Skis with a large tip have the running length further back than those with a shorter tip, in which case the boot should, theoretically, be mounted further back.

4. Generally speaking, a boot that is mounted further forward will make the ski easier to turn, and a boot mounted further back will make the ski feel more stable in a straight line.

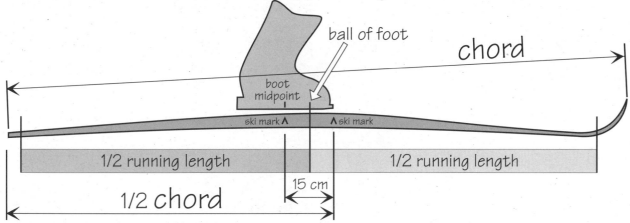

2. POSITIONING THE TOEPIECE

Once you have established where the boot will sit on the ski, slip the toepiece of the binding under the boot, and clearly mark on the ski where the toepiece is to be positioned.

3. MARKING HOLE POSITIONS FOR TOEPIECES

a) Measure up the hole positions for the toepiece and mark these on the ski with a scriber and rule. A high degree of care and accuracy is necessary to position the holes correctly.

b) Use the scriber to make a small indent where the holes are to be drilled.

c) Use a centre punch (or, better still a finger drill) to mark the hole positions more substantially.

d) Place the binding on the ski to check the marked out positions.

e) Put the boot in the toepiece to check the boot and ski alignment marks are still in line.

f) Mark out the second ski in the same way, or by taking measurements from the first ski. Then repeat checks (d) & (e).

4. DRILLING HOLES FOR THE TOEPIECES

a) Drill toepiece holes in both skis to the correct diameter and depth.

b) Countersink all holes with a countersink tool. This helps to prevent the surface of the ski bulging when the screws are inserted. If the ski bulges, the binding will not sit flat on the top of the ski.

c) If you have a thread-cutting tap, tap the holes.

5. MOUNTING THE TOEPIECES

If your binding has a connecting band between the toepiece and heelpiece, check to see if any of the parts need to be fixed to the toepiece before it is screwed to the ski.

Squirt waterproof woodworking adhesive in the screw holes. Screws can still be removed with this type of adhesive if need be.

Use a number 3 pozidrive screwdriver to mount the toepieces to skis.

Note: A number 2 pozidrive or other type of cross-head screwdriver will probably damage the screws, and may not allow you to tighten the screws sufficiently.

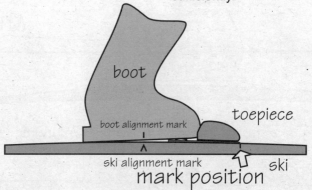

boot

toepiece

boot alignment mark

ski alignment mark

ski

mark position

6. POSITIONING THE HEELPIECES

a) The heelpiece has adjustment for different sized boots. Set the adjustment to a **central** position to allow for any position errors.

b) With the boot in the toepiece, mark where the **open** heelpiece should sit on the ski. If you need the binding to fit smaller or larger sized boots than the one being used for alignment, you may want to consider mounting the heelpiece slightly forward or backward.

  Note 1: Don't measure the position with the heelpiece closed otherwise you will mount the binding too far back. This is because there will be no tension on the spring in the heelpiece when holding it by hand, giving a false position.

  Note 2: If bindings have a band that connects the toepiece to the heelpiece, check that it will all fit together with the heelpiece in this position.

7. MARKING HOLE POSITIONS FOR HEELPIECES

a) Mark out the hole positions for the heelpieces in a similar way to the toepieces.

b) Check for correct hole positions in the same way too.

8. DRILLING HOLES FOR THE HEELPIECES

a) Drill holes.

b) Countersink holes.

c) If you have a thread-cutting tap, tap the holes.

9. MOUNTING THE HEELPIECES

If your binding has a connecting band between the toepiece and heelpiece, check to see if any of the parts need to be fixed to the heelpiece before it is screwed to the ski.

  Screw down using glue, as you did with the toepiece.

10. SETTING UP THE BINDING TO YOUR BOOTS

Follow manufacturer's guidelines to adjust the various settings on the binding to fit your boot.

11. SETTING UP THE RELEASE SETTINGS

Follow manufacturer's guidelines to set the safety release settings appropriate to the skier. These settings are governed by an ISO standard (see inside front cover of book for release chart).

12. BEFORE USING THE BINDING

Before using the binding make the maintenance and safety checks on page 120.

STRIPPED THREADS

If any threads become stripped, the hole can be drilled to a larger size and a helicoil glued in place.

heelpiece
(open)

boot

toepiece

mark position

ski

Fixing Poles

Poles may have to be straightened, shortened, or have their baskets replaced.

TOOLS
- Vice
- Pozidrive screwdriver
- Hacksaw
- 3 square (triangle) file
- Hammer
- Block of wood with hole

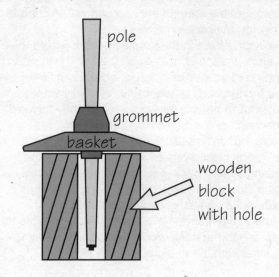

pole

grommet

basket

wooden
block
with hole

STRAIGHTENING POLES

Aluminium poles sometimes bend in a fall. It may be possible to straighten them without cracking them by bending them over a large radius object with a soft but firm surface. Bending them around a sharp corner will almost certainly snap them, or at least weaken them. After straightening, check for cracking or any other signs of weakness.

SHORTENING POLES

You may need to shorten your ski poles. To calculate correct length, read page 124.
1. Undo the screw at the top of the handle.
2. Use a piece of wood to tap off the handle.
3. Cut off the required amount with a hacksaw.
4. Remove all burrs caused by sawing.
5. Remove plastic plug (if there is one) from sawn-off section of pole.
6. Insert the plastic plug in the top of the pole, then secure it as you found it.
7. Replace the handle and secure with a screw.
  Remember you can always chop a bit off, but you can't...

REPLACING BASKETS

Baskets may fall off, or become damaged.
  The basket is held in place with a small grommet. The grommet is pressed onto the pole and the basket is pressed onto the grommet.
  Replacing the basket or the grommet is easier if you make up a pressing tool, such as a piece of wood with a hole in it.
  If the basket is damaged, remove it and fit another basket, ensuring it matches the grommet. Put the ski tip into the hole in the wooden block and tap the handle of pole (protect the handle) to secure the basket on the grommet.
  To replace the grommet, use the wooden block and a hammer to secure it.

GENERAL TIPS

CARRYING SKIS

There is a knack to carrying skis easily.

Tip 1: skis are easiest to carry over the shoulder with tips pointing forward and bindings behind the shoulder.

Tip 2: pick them up by positioning both hands in front of the bindings and pointing both thumbs towards the tails. Then swing them up onto your shoulder.

Tip 3: ski brakes are designed to be interlocked together; this prevents skis sliding apart.

STANDING UP AFTER A FALL

Tip 1: if one ski has come off, position yourself with your ski-less leg on the uphill side **before** you stand up. This makes it easier to get your ski back on.

Tip 2: position your skis across the fall line to stop you sliding downhill when you stand up.

Tip 3: in deep snow, grasp the middle of both poles in one hand, then push against them to stand up.

PUTTING SKIS ON AFTER A FALL

Tip 1: if your ski has released from the toepiece, the heelpiece of your binding will be closed. Open (prime) it manually before putting your boot back in.

Tip 2: clear out any snow from your bindings, so that your boot is unhindered.

Tip 3: in deep snow, trample a space to put your skis on so snow cannot drop into the bindings.

Tip 4: when both skis have come off, it can be difficult to put on your downhill ski. A useful trick is a leg-crossing technique. Place one ski on the snow, uphill of both your legs. Then cross your downhill leg in front of your uphill leg and into the binding, while using your poles for balance. You can now easily put on your uphill ski.

Tip 5: your ski pole is a useful tool for cleaning off snow from the base of your boot. The pole can be used in two ways. Lift your foot and tap your pole against your boot to knock off loose snow, or scrape off more persistent snow by running the middle of the pole along the base of your boot. Have the tip of the pole planted in the snow while you do this, so you can apply pressure to scrape off snow effectively.

SKI POLE BRAKE

Ski pole braking gives you a second chance to stop if you find yourself sliding down a slope after falling over. This technique is only possible when wrist loops aren't used; I never use them. To brake, throw away one pole so you have one hand free. Grab the middle of the other pole with this hand. Take your hand from the top of the pole and place it just above the basket. You can now use the tip of the pole to slow you down. Try to place the whole of your body's weight over it.

GENERAL TIPS

FINDING SKIS IN POWDER

When skiing in deep powder you can lose your skis, usually for just a minute, sometimes for half an hour or more and occasionally until the spring thaw. This is the last thing you need on a powder day when the skiing is just magic.

Tip 1: powder cords are 1.5 metre lengths of thin cord or ribbon that help you locate your skis when they come off. Attach the cords to the heelpiece of your binding in a place that won't interfere with their function. Stuff the other ends of the cords up your trouser legs. When a ski comes off, the cord unravels to make the ski easier to find.

Don't tie the cord to your leg. If you are attached to the ski by such a cord, it increases the likelihood of injury. Powder cords are different from the old fashioned powder leashes, which were used in the early days instead of ski brakes. Leashes were much shorter and were attached to the lower leg.

Only use cords on a powder day because although they are helpful in finding skis, they are inconvenient.

Tip 2: before searching for a ski, mark your position with a ski pole. You can soon trample down a large area of snow when searching and this quickly makes it impossible to recall exactly where it was you fell. You may then waste time searching in places where the ski is unlikely to be.

Tip 3: before you start your search, try to remember when it was that your ski came off. Was it your ski coming off that caused the fall, or did it come off after a couple of tumbles? Usually your ski will be above you; sometimes it may carry on sliding through the powder and end up below you. Look for any telltale signs on the surface of the snow below you. But remember, a ski may end up below you even though there are no visible signs on the surface. You realise this after fifteen minutes or so!

Tip 4: search in a criss-cross pattern, using the tail of your other ski or your pole.

SKIING OUT-OF-BOUNDS AND IN THE BACKCOUNTRY

If you want to venture out-of-bounds at a ski resort, or into the backcountry, it becomes necessary to learn about snow at a much deeper level so you can travel more safely through avalanche-prone terrain. You will be looking at the snow crystals through a magnifying glass as well as at a distance. The details of avalanches fall outside the scope of this book, but I will mention one point here.

It is very tempting to ski just outside the boundary of a skifield. But be warned, the snow conditions are much much different outside the ski area. Why is this? Inside the ski area, each fresh layer that forms is stabilised either by the ski patrol using explosives, or by skiers creating a **'skier modified surface'**. Constant skier traffic chops up new snow which stabilises it. Beyond the ski area boundary, there are no patrols using explosives and insufficient skiers to modify the surface. Therefore, what might be perfectly safe skiing in-bounds might be highly dangerous just ten metres beyond the boundary fence.

Remember too that avalanches do happen within ski areas, even on a skier modified surface. And what may be stable one day could be unstable the next (stability can often change dramatically within the hour).

SKIING IN FLAT LIGHT

Flat light is caused by clouds diffusing the light, so few shadows are cast on the snow, making it appear as an even shade of white. This makes it impossible to see the ups and downs of the snow's surface. But people, trees and buildings can easily be seen.

Tip 1: if there are trees to the side of the piste, ski beside them. The trees cast a faint shadow on the snow, making it easier to see the surface.

Tip 2: if you are competent enough and there are skiable forests, take to the trees where the visibility is nearly always better.

Tip 3: follow behind another skier who acts as an indicator of what's in front.

SKIING IN A WHITEOUT

Whiteouts occur when the sky is overcast and it is snowing. In a whiteout you cannot distinguish between the snow on the ground and the snow in the air; they both merge together. This distorts your senses e.g. you may think you are standing still when you are moving. You usually discover this when you unexpectedly fall over; this can be confusing and amusing.

   When conditions are this bad, you are usually on your way back to the cafe. To get there you can take a few extra precautions:

Tip 1: ski slowly.

Tip 2: ski a few turns at a time, then stop, get a sense of where you are and carry on.

Tip 3: if you are skiing with a friend or group, organise yourselves to stop every four or five turns (depending on the visibility), so you keep together and in sight of each other.

Tip 4: if there are only two of you, and you are organised, you can use a leapfrog technique to stay together. Leapfrogging enables you to ski twice the visible distance without stopping, while remaining in sight of each other. The trick is to ski one at a time, with each skier stopping **ahead** of the other. For example if you can see four turns ahead, ski four turns past your buddy. That way each of you skis eight turns before stopping (after the initial four turns to start the system). This makes it quicker to get out of the weather. This leapfrogging principle can be extended with more people but entropy often reigns.

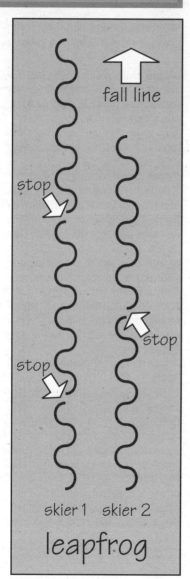

fall line

stop

stop

stop

skier 1   skier 2

leapfrog

GLOSSARY

Most definitions of skiing terms are within the text of the book, and are indexed. The index directs you to this page for definitions not given elsewhere.

Alpine skiing: skiing with the toe and heel attached to the ski; also called recreational or downhill skiing.

Avalanche (in skiing context): movement of a section of snowpack down a mountainside. Speed can vary from slow to faster than an express train. Size can vary, from too small to bury a person to large enough to bury a village.

Boiler plate: rock-hard ice.

Canting: the use of wedges (cants) between the binding and the ski. Canting enables knock-kneed and bowlegged skiers to position their knees centrally (or just inside of centre) over the ski. Canting is used by racers to increase performance. Whether canting is worthwhile for recreational skiers is debatable.

Chute: narrow strip of snow between bands of rock.

Cuff adjustment: adjustment of the cuff angle to the boot shell, to match the angle of your leg. Because the cuff wraps around the outside of the shell, the effectiveness of cuff adjustment is debatable, some designs are better than others.

Note that cuff adjustment is different to canting using cants.

DIN: Deutsche Industrie Normen (German Industrial Standards).

DIN setting: term often used to refer to the binding release setting. Note that release setting is governed by international standard ISO 11088 (see inside front cover).

Edging: tilting skis onto their edges.

Frostbite: freezing of surface and deeper tissue. Looks white and feels frozen and numb. Frostbite typically affects fingers and toes. Remove constrictions such as rings. Move patient to a warm place and warm the area carefully. Never rub, nor expose skin to hot objects. The re-warming is very painful, so painkillers are needed.

Frostnip: freezing of surface tissue only, usually to exposed skin, e.g. ears, nose, fingers, and face. Looks white and feels tender. Area must be rewarmed as soon as possible to prevent development of frostbite.

Hardpack: hard snow surface.

Heli skiing: using helicopters instead of ski lifts to reach the top of a slope.

Helicoils: if a thread in a ski becomes stripped, the hole can be enlarged with a drill and a helicoil insert added. The helicoil provides a normal screw thread.

ISO: International Organisation for Standardisation.

Lateral Stability: sideways balance.

Off piste: terrain that is off the groomed runs at a ski resort.

Piste: the groomed runs at a ski resort.

Powder hounds: skiers who love powder skiing.

Roll over: where the angle of terrain steepens to form a convex shaped slope.

Scissoring: occurs when ski edges cross over each other, blunting the edges.

Tail hopping: lifting your ski tails excessively when making pivoted parallel turns.

Tracked out: after a fresh snowfall the mountains are free from ski tracks. The term tracked out is used when there is no more untracked snow to ski.

Tracking it out: skiing untracked new snow and leaving tracks.

Trail: the groomed runs at a ski resort.

Tree line: the altitude above which trees cannot grow.

Wipe out: a fall.

This index also includes additional references to pages that may be useful, even though the exact word may not be mentioned on that page.

INDEX

INDEX